H50 243 826 9

Hertfordshire
COUNTY COUNCIL
Community Information

7/12

D1491690

2 9 JAN

- 7 AUG 2000

2 8 OCT 2000

- 1 AUG 2001
1 4 FEB 2002

B/ROC

Please renew/return this item by the last date shown.

So that your telephone call is charged at local rate,
please call the numbers as set out below:

	From Area codes 01923 or 020:	From the rest of Herts:
Renewals:	01923 471373	01438 737373
Enquiries:	01923 471333	01438 737333
Minicom:	01923 471599	01438 737599

L32

CIRCULATING STOCK ROUTE _____ 17

free spirits

BY THE SAME AUTHOR

The British Ethical Societies

F.R. Leavis: A Life in Criticism

F.R. Leavis: Essays and Documents (with Richard Storer)

free spirits

Henri Pierre Roché, François Truffaut
and the Two English Girls

IAN MACKILLOP

BLOOMSBURY

Hertfordshire Libraries, Arts and Information

H50 243 826 9

BC	06/00
B/ROC	£16-99
843/ROC	

Grateful acknowledgement is made to the following for permission
to reprint previously published material: André Dimanche: *Ecrits sur l'art* (1998),
Carnets Années Jules et Jim (1990). Editions Gallimard: *Les Deux Anglaises et le Continent* (1956). Calder &
Boyars: *Jules and Jim* translated by Parick Evans (1963) reprinted by Marion Boyars, London, New York 1981.
Also to J. C. Roché for permission to reproduce original material of Henri Pierre Roché.

First published in Great Britain 2000

Copyright © 2000 by Ian MacKillop

Picture Sources

Carlton Lake Collection, Harry Ransom Humanities Research Center,
The University of Texas at Austin: pages 11, 13, 146, 158 top & bottom

Tate Gallery, London 1999: page 37

P. Zucca/Kipa: pages 86 & 178

With kind permission of Kika Markham: page 179

Every reasonable effort has been made to ascertain and acknowledge
the ownership of copyrighted photographs illustrations and text included in
this volume. Any errors that have inadvertently occurred will be corrected
in subsequent editions provided notification is sent to the publisher.

The moral right of the author has been asserted

Bloomsbury Publishing Plc, 38 Soho Square, London W1V 5DF

A CIP catalogue record is available from the British Library

ISBN 0 7475 4855 2

10 9 8 7 6 5 4 3 2 1

Typeset by Hewer Text Ltd, Edinburgh
Printed in Great Britain by Clays Ltd, St Ives plc

For Rosie Ford

The world is full of orphans: firstly, those
   Who are so in the strict sense of the phrase
(But many a lonely tree the loftier grows
   Than others crowded in the forest's maze);
The next are such as are not doomed to lose
   Their tender parents in their budding days,
But merely their parental tenderness,
Which leaves them orphans of the heart no less.

The next are 'only children', as they are styled,
   Who grow up children only, since the old saw
Pronounces that an 'only''s a spoilt child.
   But not to go too far, I hold it law
That where their education, harsh or mild,
   Trangresses the great bounds of love or awe,
The sufferers, be't in heart or intellect,
Whate'er the cause are orphans in effect.

Byron

There are three sexes, men, women, and English girls;
and I want English girls.

Jules Laforgue

CONTENTS

Preface

Free Spirits is about the triangular relationship of three young people, two English sisters (Margaret and Violet Court) and a Frenchman (Henri Pierre Roché), between 1899 and 1914, and about the film director François Truffaut's fascination with their story many years later. Out of the four it was Roché who lived longest: he died at the age of eighty in 1959. The sisters died in 1926 and 1950 at the ages of forty-seven and seventy. Truffaut died at the age of fifty-two in 1984. Henri Pierre Roché is known today largely by association with Truffaut, though his reputation as an art critic and collector, novelist and diarist is increasing as his works come slowly off the press in beautifully edited French and German editions. He has made occasional appearances in the biographies of people he knew in the world of art, for example, Duchamp, Picasso and the American patron of artists and writers John Quinn. In 1999 he was the subject of a thorough biography by Scarlett and Philippe Reliquet.

Up to now Roché's popular reputation has been that of the man who wrote the novel *Jules and Jim* of which Truffaut made a film at once vivacious and grim in 1962. *Jules and Jim* was based on Roché's life immediately before the 1914–1918 war. Its heroes, both writers, mix with artists of all kinds and live as bohemians or free spirits. The central figure in the novel and in their lives is Catherine, memorably played by Jeanne Moreau in the film. She is the freest spirit of all and as lover is shared by Jules and Jim. Truffaut liked the novel when he first read it because of the way it showed what he called an 'aesthetic morality'. He meant that the characters in the novel try to fashion a unique moral shape for themselves as if, though persons, they are works of art. It is difficult to make a satisfactory analogy between a person and work of art, but it is easy to see the attractions of the desire to do this and how the analogy was made in the liberating years at the turn of the century. Henri Pierre Roché was the 'Jim' of the novel and his friend Franz Hessel was 'Jules'.

The novel *Jules and Jim* did not rely entirely and vicariously on the popularity of Truffaut's film. It enjoyed enough success when it was published in 1953 to encourage Roché to write a second novel, an unusual undertaking for a man already in his seventies. His next novel, *Two English Girls and the Continent*, was also autobiographical, describing an earlier period of his life, beginning in 1899, focusing upon himself and the two English sisters, Margaret and Violet, who were his first serious loves. The trio are the free spirits in the title of this book and Pierre, Margaret and Violet are its subject, as is Truffaut's relationship to their story. Roché and Truffaut of course appear under their own names; Violet and Margaret were the sisters' real first names, but I have invented the surname 'Court'. I explain the reason for this in Sources and Acknowledgements at the end.*

Roché's *Two English Girls and the Continent* was published in 1956 and Truffaut filmed it too, though not until 1971, the culmination of his long-standing fascination with it. The novel was based on Roché's memories, on his diaries, and on the letters and diaries of the two English girls themselves which Roché owned either because he was the recipient or because they had been sent to him by Margaret Court who sympathised with his belief that 'an account of our difficulties would be useful to others'. This novel was more experimental than *Jules and Jim*, appearing (only appearing) to be a weave of actual journal entries and extracts from letters.

I will be showing how their lives mingled as a result of

---

* See Sources and Acknowledgments, p. 205.

my explorations among Roché's papers, the sisters' papers and Roché's novel about them. They will appear in various incarnations as Margaret, Violet and Pierre (reality) and Muriel, Anne and Claude (fiction). I have tended to call Roché by the name of 'Pierre' for his young self and 'Roché' for the man and novelist who looked back. Truffaut's film had the same name as *Two English Girls and the Continent* (or nearly so: he added 'the'), but I have called it *Anne and Muriel*, the name of the English sub-titled version, so it will not be confused with the novel. *Free Spirits* is about three distinct periods: the years 1899 to 1914 when Pierre Roché was involved with the sisters, the late 1950s when Truffaut discovered Roché's work and befriended the man himself, and some months before and during 1971 when Truffaut planned and made his film of *Two English Girls and the Continent*.

It might be expected that I am about to say that *Free Spirits* gives the real story, the one behind the fiction. This is not the case. I am telling *a* story. Roché certainly simplified what happened in his novel and I have given a longer, fuller and in some respects richer version – though not in a work of art like his novel. The young Roché and the sisters experienced and thought much more than appears in the novel written by the elderly Roché, which was driven by its own particular artistic and moral priorities. But I have not switched back and forth from fiction to fact, as if revealing the truth. I have aimed to make *one* story out of the surviving materials which include the novel, parts of which sometimes help to fill a gap. I have explained this as I go along. Occasionally I have (I hope innocuously) invented something in order to avoid distracting speculation. For example, when Violet first meets Pierre in his mother's apartment, she may have been his mother's lodger, but we cannot be sure. If she was, there would be ramifications, such questions as why she hadn't met Pierre earlier. To avoid such incidental worries I have given Violet a room elsewhere in Paris in a property owned by Mme Roché.

The story of Pierre and the sisters told in Chapters One, Two and Three is based on Roché's published writings, his papers and the sisters' papers, all preserved in the Roché archive at a research library in Austin, Texas. Chapter Four shows what happened to Roché after he was separated from the sisters, sketching his life up to the point where he wrote his novel about them. In Chapter Five we return to the main matter, the English girls and Roché, and see how they entered the life of François Truffaut, posthumously in the case of the sisters. The Epilogue shows how Roché settled his accounts with the story of the trio.

Why, it might be asked, is the story worth telling? This is probably best not answered by me, at least at this point, but I could mention several things that attracted me to it. It is a classic love story, meaning it is a 'standard' story about love, even though it is about a curious love-triangle: two sisters loving and being loved by one man. (This situation is perhaps more common than one might think. In the course of writing this book I have found that anecdotes flow when I mention its subject.) It reminds us of what we think 'romantic love' is. I like the story also because such contrary elements meet in it. There is obviously England and France, but many other strands cross unexpectedly, names one would not expect to find on successive pages: Picasso and G. F. Watts; Nietzsche and Canon Henry Scott Holland; Montparnasse and Whitechapel; Anthony Trollope and Jules Laforgue; Émile Zola and Elizabeth Barrett Browning. The story shows that muddle of culture which later, with hindsight, becomes layered, filtered at best by scholarship and at worst by fashion or knowingness.

A few years ago I became very absorbed in, and wrote a book about, the lives and activities of late Victorian and Edwardian humanists or secularists, some of whom started what they called ethical societies. The 'ethical movement' faded away or reformed, partly because of the rise of socialism. I knew a lot about the ideas, quarrels and campaigns of the ethicists, but not much about the intimate lives of these people who were in some ways like Margaret Court. I never thought I would encounter such a person as Pierre Roché who was arguably at the centre of European culture in his time, but also knew about and visited ethical societies and the fraternal organisation Toynbee Hall, as well as Gertrude Stein and the Symbolist poet Maksimilian Voloshinov. These figures and many others have a fleeting presence through the coming pages, deliberately fleeting to accord with the taste of Henri Pierre Roché.

I was also attracted to this story because it concerns the well-known and the little-known, those who were 'names' and those to whom George Eliot refers at the end of *Middlemarch: A Study of Provincial Life* as having hidden lives which rest in 'unvisited tombs'. I wanted to write about hidden lives in the context of known ones – hidden lives of a certain sort: people who defied convention with little social or institutional support from class or education. Margaret and Violet Court proceeded from a village in rural Kent to the overwhelming *mêlée* of the modern world of art and new morals. They joined, briefly or wholeheartedly, bohemia. New ideas, channelled through Henri Pierre Roché, rushed torrentially upon them. I wanted to study them because they were not, so to say, members of an official bohemia, like the socially well-placed members of Bloomsbury, or the culturally knowledgeable, salaried university world. When studying the Court papers a friend said these 'sounded like D. H. Lawrence women'. Yes, they were, but they even lacked the celebrity of being fictional.

The title, *Free Spirits*, is a common phrase, but here it specifically refers to Nietzsche's use of it in the first edition of *Human, All Too Human*, published in 1876. (Nietzsche was a guiding light for Pierre Roché.)

> It may be conjectured that the decisive event for a spirit in which the type of the 'free spirit' is one day to ripen to sweet perfection has been a *great separation*, and that before it, he was probably all the more a bound spirit, and seemed to be chained for ever to his corner, to his post. What binds most firmly? Which cords can almost not be broken?

Pierre Roché and the English girls were 'bound spirits' who tried to be free, with near-tragic results for one of them. We see them as very *young* people: this must never be forgotten, though one often does tend to ignore age and chronology once a book gets going. They were young people inventing themselves for a world they had just started to notice. They were trying to do everything differently, in their own way and in pain. Truffaut was attracted to their story because he believed it showed how dreadful life can be for those in their early twenties. While bound in some ways, in others they were untethered. Both Pierre and the Courts came from families without a father, and it is possibly significant that Pierre was an only child, a kind of orphan as understood by Byron in Canto XVII of *Don Juan*, which provides one of the two epigraphs for *Free Spirits*. The other is by Jules Laforgue, the young master poet who died at twenty-seven years old in 1887 and was a near-contemporary of Roché and the two English girls. He inspired many writers, including T. S. Eliot whose 'The Love Song of J. Alfred Prufrock' is a poem in the Laforgue vein. Pierre Roché never quite communicated his enthusiasm for Laforgue to Margaret and Violet.

I must say that I am intensely indebted to the biographers, editors and librarians who have made it their business to care for the surviving papers of Roché, Truffaut and the Court sisters. For their work and other acknowledgments, see Sources and Acknowledgments.

All translations in this book are my own. So that the textual style of *Free Spirits* will not be distracting, let me say that foreign words are italicised in the usual way, but quoted foreign words are placed between inverted commas. I have called Roché 'Henri Pierre Roché' with no hyphen between his initials because this is how he wrote his name and 'Pierre' because this is what the sisters called him. As I said, by 'Pierre' I usually mean the young man and by 'Roché' the man and novelist who remembered himself when he was growing up.

Chapter One

the trio

In the spring of 1899 Mme Clara Roché introduced her son Henri Pierre to an English girl called Violet Court. The meeting took place in the Roché flat at 99 Rue d' Arago in Paris where Pierre lived with his mother and her elderly mother. Mme Roché had been a widow for ten years and Pierre was her only child. She owned another small apartment which she had bought for investment purposes and it was there that Violet was staying. She and Pierre were both nineteen years old, Pierre slightly older, with his twentieth birthday to come at the end of May.

When Pierre met Violet he was on crutches, having torn the ligaments of both knees in a fall from a garden trapeze. He had been showing off to some children during the Easter holidays. He was a good athlete who boxed and fenced like many young intellectuals, and boasted that he was 'Monsieur Jarrets d'Acier' – Mr Steel-Knees. This time he had over-reached himself.

Pierre was ordered to stay in convalescent semi-isolation at home with his mother, cut off from college, cafés, artists' studios and the girl-friends who could not be invited home to Rue d'Arago which he tersely called 'Arago'. Violet Court differed in several ways from these girls, the differences coalescing for Pierre into the fact of her being English. Violet was in Paris for a few weeks to find out about enrolling at an art school and soon was able to study painting at one of the best, the Colarossi. Young women, including young English women, quite often went to study art in Paris, so Violet's was not such a bohemian scheme as it may appear. Mme Roché was able to give her a little protection and encouraged Violet to get to know Pierre. She was acquainted with Violet's mother Emma, also a widow, who may have travelled in Germany with her husband when he was alive and (we cannot be sure) met Mme Roché as a result.

On the first sighting Pierre did not pay much attention to Violet. Mme Roché had invited her into her drawing-room to join a party for several of Pierre's friends. Pierre had only just returned from the vacation which had ended with his accident. He noticed across the room this dark-haired stranger whom he thought boyish-looking. She returned his nod with a frank smile after which his mother performed the courtesies. He wrote later in a diary that Violet was neither as pretty nor as vivacious as an average French girl, but she had a decided and responsible manner. She was, he wrote in French, 'sensible'. He could have said *sympatique*. She was less opinionated than the few English girls he had met. She used an eyeglass with a handle, a lorgnette. When she lowered it Pierre had the impression of 'a modest and pleasing nudity'.

Pierre had to rest up for long hours on his bed or a sofa which Violet later was allowed to visit, standing a decorous two paces away, for conversation. She was a proficient visitor: on arrival she would invariably return to the topic discussed at her last appearance. Their meetings, speaking in French and English by turns, had something of the character of tutorials for Violet. Pierre was a sophisticate in his own territory, and when his physician allowed him to escort Violet to galleries, parks and the theatre, he taught her about the new wave in art, especially Rodin's statue *Balzac*, which at first she thought shockingly distorted. Pierre was studying at the École des Sciences Politiques, but also went to an art school, the Académie Julian. He appears in a surviving group photograph marked 'Julian 1898', taken in one of its studios not long before he met Violet. About twenty men are posed for the camera around a naked female model with her chest out, the men affectionately close up to her neck, shoulders and breasts. A few wear painting smocks, but most are in serge suits and are probably instructors. Pierre looks the youngest and lankiest; he too is suited, his red hair brushed straight up on his head. He took Violet to *Louise*, the opera by Gustave Charpentier which had recently been premièred to great acclaim. They saw it twice and argued about its 'immorality', as judged by Violet. In it Louise, a young seamstress, sets up home with her lover Julien in spite of the fierce opposition of her mother. She returns to her family when her father is sick, her parents believing she will now renounce Julien and bohemian Paris, but she refuses and is turned out of doors by her father, even though he is more indulgent than her mother. Louise and Julien suffered from a dominant mother as did Pierre. Mme Roché was to shape his destiny, and the destinies of Violet and her sister Margaret who soon enters their story. It was said that in Charpentier's *Louise* it was Paris itself, the legendary City of Light and smoothly paved streets, which was the major protagonist that triumphed finally over bourgeois morality. Violet was fascinated by the drama, but could not agree with Pierre that some beings are above the laws of the family.

Violet talked about England. The couple shared a taste for the paintings of Edward Burne-Jones, and especially for a painting by George Frederic Watts called *Hope* which Violet loved and Pierre had seen in lithograph form: a young woman seated on a terrestrial globe, blindfolded and holding a lyre with a broken string. Was this Violet a British Louise, he wondered, a Louise who had never known Paris? Was *Hope* a portrayal of Violet?* Pierre was hungry to see England. He wrote in his diary that he was determined to experience the contradictions of this land of personal self-effacement and national pride, of conformism and Shakespeare, of the Bible and whisky. He wanted to see for himself the mixture of staidness and boldness he liked in Violet. And she encouraged him with an intriguing prospect. She said, 'I am an ordinary bourgeois English girl, but you must meet my sister. Margaret is a bit older than me and ever so much brighter. I only paint, but she is marvellous at everything. They call her

* Later Pierre and the sisters talked about *Hope*: see p. 37 on which the painting is reproduced.

our "ray of sunshine" in the village.' She showed Pierre a photograph of Margaret at the age of thirteen. 'What's she like now?' he asked. Margaret Court was twenty-one – a little older than Pierre.

Pierre persuaded Mme Roché that they should take a holiday in England. Mrs Court was delighted to have them and there the famous Margaret was to become as interested in Pierre as he had been in Violet. She made up a nickname for him. When he came down to breakfast the girls would laugh and say, 'Bonjour la France!' Margaret decided it should be different.

> Not just France. He has taught us about *Don Quixote* and Dante. He has brought Greece to life. He has given us Schopenhauer, and Knut Hamsun, and Ibsen and Tolstoy. The Court sisters will compliment him with the title he deserves. From now on we will greet him with, 'Bonjour le Continent!'

This is how the story of Pierre Roché and the two English girls began. Before seeing how it developed, let us look into the background of Pierre, this young ambassador who brought Europe to the door of the Court sisters.

Henri Pierre Roché was born in Paris on 28 May 1879. His father, Pierre Roché, was a pharmacist by profession, and a Protestant by faith, as was his wife, Clara Coquet, whom he met when she worked in a bookshop. He was an art-lover by temperament. One afternoon in the early spring of 1879, when Clara was far into pregnancy, they sat by the Medici fountain in the Luxembourg Gardens and Pierre urged her to gather up her strength for a last visit to the Louvre so that their child would love painting. In 1885, when his son was six years old, Pierre Roché senior learned he had an untreatable brain tumour: he walked swiftly to the balcony of the family apartment and died on the pavement below. Pierre was thus orphaned of his father, and his mother became a widow, photographed here a year later, in her mourning dress with jet jewellery.

Clara remained with her mother and Pierre at Arago until her death in 1929. She never remarried.

Once Pierre had taken his baccalauréat, he was rewarded by a tour of Germany with Clara where they climbed and bicycled together. He then studied law in Paris at the École des Sciences Politiques; he was, he said later, 'a Tolstoyan and a Socialist'. A friend said he looked the part of a Socialist with his red hair like Bernard Shaw's. He was tall, slim and wiry, usually unbearded, and a melancholy-looking joker: one photo album is full of crazy poses. He was friendly with Jacques Maritain, three years his junior; they wrote to each other on Socialist and humanitarian issues, especially at the time of the Belgian First of May Manifesto.

Clara Roché had aspirations for Pierre to join the diplomatic service, but was advised that he had little hope of succeeding without wealth or better connections. Her son persuaded her he could make a living from literary journalism, translation and writing about art. His professor advised him (prophetically as it transpired) that 'You are an idealist, an experimenter, a connoisseur. Forget qualifications. Travel. Write. Translate. Learn how to live anywhere. France needs *informateurs*, the sort of people they have in England.' By 'informateurs' he meant 'investigators' and by 'the sort of people they have in England' he was thinking, perhaps, of W. T. Stead, the campaigning journalist, editor of the *Pall*

Mall and author of the famous exposé of child prostitution, *The Maiden Tribute of Modern Babylon* of 1885. (After Stead's death in 1912, on the *Titanic* while travelling to a peace conference, Lord Esher said of him that 'no events happened to the country since 1880 which had not been influenced by the personality of Mr Stead'.) Pierre was attracted to the rôle of investigating sociologist, and soon, under the influence of one of the English girls, was to move to the East End of London to study in one of the worst British slums. Before this, as we saw, he had studied part-time at, or at least frequented, an art school, the Académie Julian, where he took two years to realise that he would never be a painter. The models were an attraction, though he was shy.

Pierre Roché was now on the threshold of a sexual career which had begun about the time he first ejaculated at the age of twelve, after looking at the breasts of his mother's maid in the next room at Arago, and then progressed to a girl in a side street off the Boulevard St Michel. He went with some street-girls, but said he was 'always unsatisfied' by them. With his best friend, fellow-student Jo Jouanin, Pierre devised an enterprising method of meeting women. They shared the cost of a newspaper advertisement which invited women who enjoyed discussion and human relations to meet them. It worked spectacularly: in one day alone Jo and Pierre received a hundred replies, so they rented a back room at a café to spread out the letters into categories and discuss tactics. Sometimes immediate meetings were arranged, but usually there would be correspondence. Sometimes no meeting materialised, as was the case with the exquisite green-ink calligraphist whose style reminded Pierre of Jules Laforgue; he wondered whether this handwriting actually cloaked the identity of a man. A taste for letter-writing was born, and an interest in graphology. Pierre Roché had his own handwriting analysed several times; an inked print of his right hand survives in his papers. We see here a photograph of Jo and Pierre (left) in this period, with grave expressions on their faces, on the back of which Roché wrote that it showed them discussing 'notre pièce'.

They could have been writing a play ('pièce'), but this is mentioned nowhere else so it is more likely that he was referring to the concoction of their advertisement. Before he met Violet and her sister, Pierre had four special girl-friends: Maria, Marcelle, Henriette and a married woman who occasionally visited Paris whom he called 'La Lyonnaise'. Maria was a leftist. 'What would a Socialist be like in bed? Always the question.' Marcelle was boyish and the most erotically capable. Henriette was a 'virtuous prostitute', whom he had met at the Folies Bergères. She had been disowned by her family because she would not marry their choice of husband and therefore decided to earn her living in the clubs. They had many conversations and a brief love-affair. Her plight impressed itself on Pierre as a Socialist, becoming the more important for him when he read later about the use of women as property in *Free Love* (*L'Amour Libre*) by the anarchist Charles Albert, and read Schopenhauer, who dispelled all sentimentality from Pierre about concepts of love which disguised the use of women as commodities before and after marriage. He admired Henriette, but genitally she was shaped in such a way that love-making was difficult. By the time he met Violet he was fairly experienced. 'When I was a schoolboy the idea of sex was the Absolute.' At nineteen sex was no longer a value in itself. Like many shy men he was puzzled that women appeared to give themselves to him. One girl said he was attractive because you could see how frightened he was, and he agreed: he *had to* tell women he wanted them with his fear showing. He considered himself to be moderately restrained – he liked the English word 'continent' – having worked out that in the period of Maria, Henriette, Marcelle and the lady from Lyon, he had had sex on average once every eighteen days. Roché was always a careful keeper of records. He logged his activities with Jo in a hundred pages of a journal which survives among his papers, the first specimen from Roché's lifetime practice of self-chronologising. Keeping a journal was one of three trends in the months in which he sought women with Jo. The others were sharing lovers and the enjoyment of a perpetual conversation with a close male friend.

This first journal irritated the critical eye of Roché when he re-read it in 1949 and was beginning to think of writing autobiographical fiction. He dismissed it as a 'purely sexual history'. 'What a dry testimony of a young male between realism and romanticism, searching for himself. Not a pleasant document, but useful for chronology.' The exercise-book pages have some deletions scratched across them, and once: 'Burn without reading.' It was only in 1904, at the age of twenty-five, five years after meeting the English girls, that the 'real' Roché journals begin. 'I would always have little grey, soft-covered notebooks in my pocket, in which I recorded my sessions with my painter friends and their women, evenings which sometimes lasted till dawn. For my own pleasure I would note the facts and the gestures. One hundred of these notebooks accumulated between 1904 and 1956, sometimes summaries, sometimes detailed.' He wrote this in the essay 'Around Painters in My Time' (1946), putting stress on his encounters with artists, but he also carefully recorded in the grey notebooks his own erotic life, using code words for sexual technicalities like 'Sp' (*i.e.* spend, for ejaculate), 'Tph' (*i.e.* 'touche petit homme', for masturbate)', and 'Tpf' (touching a woman's sex). He found the composition and ascetic revision of these journals deeply satisfying, a full-scale preoccupation, and indeed a life's work.

As for close male friendship and the sharing of lovers, Roché became a byword for these after *Jules and Jim*, which dramatised his relationship with Franz Hessel, a relationship which was mirrored in his later friendship with Marcel Duchamp and was established in his late teens with Jo Jouanin.

Mme Roché believed Pierre was highly-strung ('neurasthénique'). One spring he was so visibly exhausted by the first-year law examinations that she insisted he went to southern France to recuperate, so for three weeks he had to leave the girls acquired by correspondence. He decided to do Jo a favour because he had proved the less popular advertiser: he would experiment to see if anything happened between Jo and the Socialist, Maria. Would they have sex? Pierre listed his motives meticulously in his journal. He wanted to please Maria, in whom his interest was slightly fading; he wanted to set up Jo with an adventure; he wanted to have the chance of discussing Maria with Jo later and to see what Maria would do and say. Most of all, it seems that he wanted to experiment with the sensation of being cuckolded. Pierre did not explain all this to Jo, giving him only an excuse to visit: he asked Jo to return a book he had borrowed from Maria.

In his journal Pierre listed six stages of correspondence that followed between Maria, Jo and himself in the Midi. (1) Maria: Jo has delivered the books, as arranged with Pierre, (2) Jo: the books are safely delivered, (3) Jo (postcard): he is taking Maria to eat at Antoine's, (4) Maria: going to restaurant and theatre with Jo – he's so nice. Eight days later Jo writes to say he really would like to go to bed with Maria, (5) Maria: analyses the books Jo delivered: 'I am always your friend', (6) Jo: a letter with so many stamps on it that Pierre gauged from its thickness that he must be now well and truly cuckolded. Pierre kept this letter unread in his pocket for several hours. When he opened it, he found Jo faithfully describing having sex with Maria. It seemed that the love-making was similar to his and hers – and Pierre noticed he was 'not distressed' about their four sexual encounters, as counted out by Jo. What joy! His feelings were *not* hurt. He 'could mind', but thought he must 'be different', not be like the mass of men. There was some jealousy, but the thought of dissimulation repelled him.

More letters followed, beginning with a breezy one from Maria who said how much she was enjoying Jo's company. It was then her turn to send a thick envelope, whose contents explained she could not sleep if she did not confess to Pierre that she had been to bed several times with Jo. She gave hardly any detail. She loved comparing them, she said, and 'coming to no conclusion'. If only she could have a child by both and watch how each grows up differently.

About the time he met Violet, Pierre bought his first work of art, an advertising card in a shoemaker's window. It cost one franc and seventy centimes. He asked the shoemaker to sign it, a prophetic act for the man who became a friend of Marcel Duchamp, inventor of 'Readymades'. The shoemaker demurred. He did not sign shoes, so why sign this?

This is how Pierre grew up, the boy who symbolised Europe or 'The Continent' to the two English girls. In the summer of 1899 Pierre met both of them together.

Pierre left Paris with Mme Roché to follow Violet across the Channel and see Margaret, whom her sister Violet had said was so fascinating. In fact, he went not to England but to north Wales near Conway Castle to stay in a holiday cottage rented by the Courts, that is, Mrs Emma Court, Violet, Margaret and their brother Stephen.

As in Pierre's family, there was no father on the scene. While alive, Mr Court had had a good importing business with offices in London and had travelled widely. He was ten years older than his wife. Not long after their marriage, in the late 1870s, he was prosperous enough to move the family from London to Kent, into a hamlet called Kingsnorth, near Ashford, a small town in sheep-farming country and at that time just booming as a railway manufacturing plant. From Kingsnorth, the sea was sometimes just visible across Romney Marsh, twenty miles away. Ashford is still quintessentially English, now a little suburban, but aware of the proximity of France and today favoured by French businesses. It is the only cross-Channel train station south of London. Mr Court bought a substantial house on farming land which the family continued to live in when he did not return from a trading journey to Malaya, having contracted yellow fever. So Margaret, Violet and Stephen were orphaned of a father, like Pierre, before the age of ten.

Pierre and his mother were welcomed in Wales in 1899, but the visit began awkwardly. At this time there was strong anti-French feeling in Britain because of the Fashoda Incident. (Britain and France had been on the brink of war after a French expedition impudently and heroically advanced up the Nile valley on to 'British' territory, to be blocked by Kitchener in the autumn of 1898.) Stephen was at Cambridge and sufficiently up-to-date with current affairs to regard Pierre warily, though he also felt a more primitive hostility to a foreign man striding the turf of his all-female family. Excuses were made for Margaret, who was unwilling to make an appearance: she was ill and had trouble with her sight, so Pierre was thrown into Violet's easy-going company. She took him out after dark to the huge estuary below Conway Castle at low tide and now explained that Margaret, despite her gifts, was 'not strong'. Violet's rôle model was evidently less dynamic than Pierre had expected. Violet readily visited the castle with him, which nearby had the attraction of a hall of mirrors in which they got lost: Pierre panicked, or pretended to do so, and Violet therefore took him by the shoulders and frog-marched him to safety. Pierre thought this was a cue for kissing even for an English girl, but Violet seemed unconscious of sexual attraction. After a few days Margaret appeared, red-haired, quick-witted and serious. She joined in everything and one of them said (they never remembered who) that they were a trio. Margaret wore a crêpe eye-bandage some of the time. She was, and should not have been, a late-night reader by candle-light, especially of Darwin and the Darwinians. She talked about how evolutionary change could be accelerated to diminish the sufferings of the industrial poor. She was the devout one of the family, as well as being almost tiringly vivacious. Violet by comparison acted gauchely, even sullenly, in company. Stephen taught Pierre cricket; there was charades and naked sea-bathing, with the girls further up the shore. Margaret wore her bandage less frequently, using tinted spectacles instead, and practised golf strokes. The trio began language lessons for each other, and read aloud. They pledged friendship, and swore they would always tell each other the truth. They went climbing. Pierre, whose knees were still painful, trailed behind, more than strictly necessary because he liked watching the soft white nape of Margaret's neck below her red-gold hair. (She had her father's hair.) He called her 'Nuk', standing for 'sa nuque', then and long afterwards, even after they had parted. Thenceforth red-haired women, the 'Rousses', always interested him.

During this first holiday it was Pierre and Violet who were teased for being inseparable, rather than Pierre and Margaret. Mrs Court worried that Margaret was being left out, which would be the worse if she took a fancy to Pierre. Stephen was jealous on Margaret's behalf because he thought irritably it was Violet to whom Pierre was attracted. Mme Clara Roché thought that Pierre was safe with the plainer Violet. The girls seemed boisterously unaware of such possibilities. Not to be outdone by her sister, Margaret also took Pierre in hand for another visit to the maze of mirrors, before he went home. She led him through more swiftly, and held his hand more tightly. Pierre thought his chest was going to burst. He could not stop thinking about how his experience of the sisters had been replicated in the dark – and about how the sisters appeared truly to believe that he could be their brother.

In October 1899 the Court family decamped to Paris where they furnished an apartment with market and makeshift pieces of furniture, to stay until the spring of 1900. There were now plenty of opportunities to know Pierre better. The girls enrolled for some courses at the Sorbonne. Sporting activities continued. Even Mrs Emma Court was reading, and penetrated *Les Misérables*, though only in English. Pierre told Margaret she must read Zola's *Germinal*, but she did not attempt it until later, with drastic results, as we shall see. Pierre skipped some of his own lectures and preparations at the École to spend more time with the sisters, but mainly Margaret because now Violet had seriously begun to paint and had started taking art classes.

Stephen joined them at the end of his spring term, as did various friends and relatives from England. It was the time to catch the last weeks of the Éxposition Universelle. There were visits to Versailles, to Sèvres, café talk, nights at the Opéra, football, cycling, *pélote*, reading the Belgian *avant garde* (Rodenbach and Maeterlinck). They looked at the Rodins: there had been over a hundred in the Éxposition which were in the course of being re-sited in the parks. Margaret was frequently embarrassed by the deficiencies of her French, painfully aware that she could not chat. Sometimes she felt nausea, blaming it on Paris milk which she vowed not to drink. Mme Roché critically noted her ailments; she suggested a few weeks in a clinic or 'maison de séclusion', definitely away from Pierre. These months saw the birth of the first love union between Pierre and the sisters, with Margaret rather than Violet. She was to become perhaps the founding love in his life, later to be compared even to Catherine of *Jules and Jim*, despite her very great differences, one of which was her lack of bohemianism – except in one respect: her regard for Pierre, as yet only just born.

While in Paris Margaret wrote a journal of her life. It was kept intermittently and undertaken partly to practise her French, only running to twenty-four sides of an exercise book. But it is a sequential whole, so it is likely that it is her only journal for this period. Many touches show how Pierre appealed to her, sometimes obliquely, sometimes directly, though delight in Paris and delight in Pierre run into each other. She describes how one night she realised that she was saying something in her sleep which she could only bring herself to write down as a row of dashes, but when she was back in England she wrote in the margin (marked '31st January 1900') that what she said was 'Pierre, je t'*aime*'. She wrote about the beauty of his eyes, his gentle explanations, things unnoticed during the holiday in Wales, when she was often ill or was required as eldest daughter to be hostess. Margaret puzzled over her feelings.

So: if this really is love, what then? Is there anything bad about love? The more one loves, the more one is loving. The more love one has in one's heart, the more there is love for God. The more love, the better a person can do his duty in this life. So, then, if it is truly, seriously, unalterably the case that I love Pierre (I really do not know), this need not be a bad thing for me.

She is acutely aware of her duty, her 'tâche'. She says something that is rare in her later writings: that her mother is irritating. 'If Pierre creates love in me, perhaps I could give some of it to mother.' Love for Pierre or a man like him, 'good, intelligent, *sympatique*', is a reciprocal part of the love of God: 'To love is divine, love is God.' Loving Pierre would augment her capacity for love. She says that now he is so close to her that it is surely only her will-power that stands in the way of her loving him.

Pierre becomes a prospect for love: indeed, everything is prospective in Margaret's journal, a vivid dream-work. On the title page she wrote: 'PRIVATE – *Do not forget that much of this belongs to the life of the imagination*' and it belongs to what she called 'la vie irréelle'. Journals are often random: this mosaic of incidents, sayings, thoughts is 'poetic', even though Margaret might not have intended it to be so, like a prose-poem in the era of prose-poems, written as if she were a character in a play by Maurice Maeterlinck. On the last page she casts herself into the rôle of 'daughter of Paris', spiritual child of the city. 'Oh Paris! I am pleading with you never to lose your magic for me! Please let me continue to be your adopted daughter. You and Pierre have created so much that is a part of me which will always be yours.' If she feels reborn it is as much to be explained by the influence of Paris as by that of Pierre. When Violet had first visited Paris and Pierre took her to Charpentier's *Louise*, he thought she could be a British Louise, brought to life by the city. Violet now was used to Paris, and spent long periods away from Margaret with her painting. It was Margaret who was coming under the spell of the City of Light as her journal shows, saturated with the colours of Paris: yellows, rose-tints, brilliant blues of school-girls' tabards, white lights shining through mists and the shocking inky black of the Seine. Nothing is done with self-conscious care for accuracy: Margaret was transported.

Violet was the sister who intended to be an artist and became one, and when Pierre looked back on the sisters, long after they had left him, he apportioned aesthetic gifts to Violet and intellectuality to Margaret, though he did say that Margaret's letters were 'Shakespearean'. But in her journal Margaret also sounds like a painter in the making. She becomes excited when she hears that Pierre is meeting a young artist from the provinces and that one of the Courts' English visitors is to stay in Paris to study painting. If she wondered whether she could go to art school like Violet, it was not for long because there was always mother to think about (she told herself). Whether or not she had a talent for painting, she was certainly an enthusiastic writer, perhaps even more of a writer than Pierre, whose earliest journals are factually interesting, but mundane as literary work.

Things which later became painful or even tragic flit across the screen of Margaret's journal without conflict. On one occasion a quarrel with Pierre is mentioned: he was exasperated at Margaret's lack of understanding and refused to go the Opéra with her to see *Louise* for a second time (so for the moment the plan was dropped), but usually issue follows issue without resolution. The tourist's conversational delight in comparing national characteristics is taken further than usual. Pierre said that though English girls behave freely, they do not read as much as French girls, shaming Margaret.

Pierre told Margaret she had to read *Moral Tales* (*Moralités Légendaires*) by Jules Laforgue, published in 1887, the year of

Laforgue's early death. He and Jo helped her by reading aloud passages from the chapter called 'Hamlet, or the Consequences of Filial Piety'. The chapter title was ominous for Margaret who always lived with or near her mother (not only because of filial piety), and for Pierre under the watchful eyes of Clara Roché. In this era it was fashionable to identify oneself with the figure of Hamlet. Even women did so: had not Sarah Bernhardt played the part? And amongst the intelligentsia Jules Laforgue was the most fashionable Modernist. His work epitomised what was shockingly new to Margaret. He had re-written classic stories, *Hamlet*, *Lohengrin* and *Salome*, recreating them with no sense that the famous, near mythological characters were immured in the past. Maeterlinck said that Laforgue's Hamlet was more like Hamlet, had more of the essence of 'Hamlet-ness', than Shakespeare's. In Laforgue's prose anything could happen. Some of his shock-effects scandalised Margaret, like Hamlet's 'strange destructive impulses' during a spree in which he kills small creatures and then laves his hands in their squashed eyes. For Margaret, and for Violet, Laforgue and his Hamlet were literary wild men, a little like Pierre and Jo, who intimated hints of the Dionysiac in their off-stage lives when they were not acting as escorts for the English visitors. Laforgue was a romantic aesthete of the 1890s, like Hamlet mordantly undeceived ('O, my prophetic soul!') by the orthodox world.

At about the time Jo and Pierre read Laforgue to Margaret, Pierre was introduced to the English-speaking world in Arthur Symons's *The Symbolist Movement in Literature* (1899). Symons declared that Laforgue's style was 'disarticulated, abstract, mathematically lyrical' with an 'icy ecstasy' and characters which were 'fantastic puppets, with an almost Japanese art of spiritual dislocation'. He quoted one of Hamlet's soliloquising reveries, a passage which gives the feel of just what it was that imparted a frisson to Margaret who was now face to face for the first time with 'The Continent'.

Perhaps I have still twenty or thirty years to live, and I shall pass that way like the others. Like the others? Oh Totality, the misery of being there no longer! Ah! I would like to set out to-morrow, and search all through the world for the most ada-mantine processes of embalming. They, too, were the little people of history, learning to read, trimming their nails, lighting the dirty lamp every evening, in love, gluttonous, vain, fond of compliments, hand-shakes, and kisses, living on bell-tower gossip, saying, 'What sort of weather shall we have tomorrow?' 'Winter has really come.' 'We have had no plums this year.' Ah! Everything is good, if it would not come to an end. And thou, Silence, pardon the Earth; the little madcap hardly knows what she is doing; on the day of the great summing-up of conscious-ness before the Ideal, she will be labelled with a pitiful *idem* in the column of the miniature evolutions of Unique Evolution, in the column of negligible quantities. To die! Evidently, one dies without knowing it, as every night one enters upon sleep. One has no consciousness of the passing of the last lucid thought into sleep, into swooning, into death.

Pierre told Margaret about the short life of Laforgue, though did not say that his increasing interest in 'Nuk' was on the model of Laforgue's obsession with English girls with red hair. There were, Laforgue said, three sexes: men, women and English girls; and he wanted English girls. (Laforgue did marry an English girl in London: 'She's as tall as you or I, but very thin and very English, decidedly English with her reddish brown hair, a red you simply can't imagine and one would never have believed existed until I saw her, pale skin, thin neck, and eyes, those eyes: you must see them.') In Paris and Berlin, where his profession was to read French to the aged Empress Augusta, he had tired of continental girls and sought 'pure', not necessarily chaste, women of whom English ones seemed the purest, though he was not usually successful with them. He decided that their purity was genetic.*

* In the Introduction to his translation of *Moral Tales*, published in 1985, William Jay Smith wrote that 'the descriptions and impressions of the natural scene in [Laforgue's] notebooks call to mind the inscape of Gerard Manley Hopkins or the poems of Elizabeth Bishop. And the freshness and charm of his letters have prompted some critics to refer to him as the French Keats.' I have used Smith's translation of the title *Moralités Légendaires* as *Moral Tales*.

Pierre made no secret of being an anarchist, an unsettling fact for Margaret who was a hard-working parish helper at home, doing her best for the rural workers, collecting rents, and believing she had her part to play in the relief of poverty. Here was Pierre with his conviction that maintaining one's own identity was morally paramount. He was sarcastic on the subject of 'going about the world doing good'. Oh, Pierre, oh, *Pierre*!' she murmured in the privacy of her journal.

The greatest difficulty for Margaret lay in accepting the way in which Pierre talked about sex – brought sex *in*to their conversations about men and women. He soon learned to tease her gently with his 'freshness' about physical attraction. He was always talking about 'amour physique', but what *was* this? 'There is no other thing', Margaret wrote in her diary, 'than true love.' He talked about 'free unions', but how could any man other than a blackguard free himself from the woman he loved? Men were not, surely, animals. Worst of all, he talked neutrally and even appreciatively of the French attitude to prostitution, about sanitary regulations, the inspection of brothels, and the social service rendered by capable madams and their charges. Did not the very existence of organised prostitution condone the evil? asked Margaret. Pierre told her he knew two young men who lived on money earned from prostitution by a girl-friend. We shall see that the issue of prostitution erupted later in their friendship with much greater intensity when Margaret realised that Pierre was a sexual being rather than a clever talker about men, women and society. But at this early stage she had only to tolerate his cleverness, and managed this with ease, even feeling superior at times. She decided she liked him because he helped her think and express herself, which included improving her French.

At the end of April the whole family was to leave Paris. Margaret was determined to see *Louise* at the Opéra the second time, and did so by herself. She hurried to the Place de l'Odéon book-shops at Pierre's bidding to buy Renan's *Vie de Jésus* and Pascal's *Pensées* from which he and Mme Roché thought she could learn a more existential Protestantism than her Church of

England piety. She bought Zola's *Germinal*, published in 1885, but still forbidding and forbidden to British readers. Pierre was eager that she should read it.

Mme Roché had watched Margaret carefully and was not pleased. We do not know very much about her from the surviving papers in the Roché archive. But we know more about her than about Emma Court, and in contrast to Emma's timidity, Clara was self-controlled and domineering. There is a vivid account of Pierre's mother as 'Mme Claire Roc' in *Two English Girls and the Continent*. The chapter entitled 'Claire' contains a few pages of 'Claire's Memories', in the first person, as told to Claude/Pierre. It is impossible to resist the belief that she was deeply possessive of her 'neurasthénique' son who still shared her apartment in Paris. She rather liked Violet to whom she later rented Pierre's old room at Arago. But she disliked the other sister intensely. When Margaret was being fitted for a dress to take home to England, she started crying because the dressmaker said she had no more figure than a baby. Significantly, Mme Roché did not reprove the woman for impertinence. She thought Margaret was a flirt and did not care for the way she would say 'my darling' in the English way to Pierre and call her sister 'good old Violet'. Margaret said she talked like this because she had never known anyone but girls and her brother Stephen. This was strange behaviour to Mme Roché. She thought Margaret was 'always ill'. She worried about her effect on Pierre whom she thought was delicate and for whom the family doctor predicted a breakdown. His mother decided he should have a spell at a sanatorium in a monastery in Sonnenberg, Alsace, and after Margaret left Paris he obediently departed. There he was subjected to a series of violent water-cures which gave him a lifelong taste for the sensuousness of icy water. He wrote, often and exhaustedly, to Margaret about little things that happened, such as the agoraphobic boy who could follow him at top speed on a bicycle, but insisted on Pierre leading him by hand across the village square.

In July 1900 the trio were reunited. Pierre and Mme Roché joined the Courts in a village in Switzerland. Violet told him by letter they could meet at a specified time in the village church. When he arrived she was there on her knees with a solemn face. A woman sighted in procession or worship, or as participant in a ceremony or performance, is a recurring motif in romance, as in Chaucer's *Troilus and Criseyde*, in which Troilus first sees Criseyde in a temple

> In widow's habit black, but natheless,
> Right as our first letter is now an 'A',
> In beautee first so stood she makeless.

In the little square outside the church Pierre once again saw her direct smile, the 'sourire franc'. He had always thought something could start with Violet and now she seemed to know it. This summer the exploits of the trio became more adventurous: shooting, climbing, braving white water. There was a scare when Stephen disappeared, only to be discovered in jail for accidentally trespassing in a reservation for mountain antelope. Mme Roché, Violet and Stephen were the first to depart, leaving Pierre, to the displeasure of his mother, with Margaret and Mrs Court. On one occasion the three of them were caught in a rainstorm while out climbing and sheltered under a bluff by a little waterfall. They squeezed together for warmth and played a Court family game called lemon squash or *citron pressé*, shaking and rocking their shoulders and elbows against each other. Pierre was dazed by this close, nearly erotic contact. He wrote a poem about the lake, the moon and Margaret which he sent to Jo who wrote back from Paris to say that Pierre was obviously in love with her. 'In love with *them*,' he replied. Mother and daughter left and Pierre went back to the flat in the Rue d'Arago. The *annus mirabilis* of 1899–1900 was over by September.

In spite of the worries about Pierre's health, he was deemed fit enough for military service and he departed for this in December 1900. Although he liked army camp life, he did not last long in the rigours of a cold Normandy winter. A fever soon confined him to the barracks hospital where at night he joined in the cabarets staged by soldiers who climbed into the sick-quarters with guitars and flagons of cider. Early in 1901 he was sent home on sick leave to Arago where his mother gave him money for an eight-day convalescent journey to the Prado in Madrid. His father would have wanted it.

He changed trains for Madrid at Burgos. The trio liked to say it had no secrets, but something happened in Burgos which Pierre only revealed in stages to the sisters.

He left Burgos station and made for the cathedral. On entering, he noticed through the gloom a beautiful young woman at prayer; she then joined a service and he saw her more clearly by candle-light speaking the responses ardently. (Here was a sighting of a girl about some sacred business, like the sighting of Violet in the Swiss church.) He managed to manoeuvre himself behind her in the communion line, watching the wafer on her fingers. He then followed her to the heavy inner door of one of the cathedral porches which, when closed, trapped them momentarily in darkness, as if in a wooden box. When they emerged into the light, the girl looked frankly at him and asked him his name. She said hers was Pilar. She motioned Pierre to follow her, which he did on a circuitous route to an apartment in a house which Pilar said belonged to a friend. He heard himself saying untruthfully that he was a virgin. Pilar was delighted to hear it, and led him to her friend's bed. She enjoyed herself so much she asked Pierre to stay in town and meet her girl-friend, the owner, who she said would also like him. She had another apartment, better than this one. Pierre was enthralled, later remembering the afternoon with Pilar as the best of love, but he said he had to go on to Madrid. He muttered that he was too Nordic for her and he had to see the Prado. Secretly he thought Pilar's friend would be a 'complication'. Pilar vanished into a crowd.

Pierre could not bring himself to tell Margaret about Pilar, but he now wrote to her about love and freedom even more passionately than when they had argued in Paris. Margaret was unpersuaded. It was a very Pierre-like communication, but so serious that Margaret did not reply in the flirtatious spirit in which she sometimes put him down. She wrote back gravely about allegiance to a chosen one:

> I believe that for each woman there is created a man, who is her husband – that though there may be several men with whom she could live a peaceful, even happy, useful life as wife – there is only one who is really her 'soul-husband'. He may be dead, she may never see him here, or he may be tied by marriage to another woman and in that case it is a pity, if the woman marries. And for each man there is somewhere one woman who can be his only perfect wife. This idea has so grown up with us since we were little children, that the other theories people have about marriage seem terrible and pitiable to me.

The life of Henri Pierre Roché was to be one of multiple loves and he saw himself correctly as a successor to Casanova. But Margaret's straightforward conviction about 'the one' impressed him deeply and he believed it was at the core of his experience of the English girls. He copied out some of these words and used them as the epigraph for *Two English Girls and the Continent*.

In the summer of 1901 Pierre was demobilised and started travelling. He was now committed to what his professor had advised: travel and observation. Margaret wrote to him in Dresden. She said he should read her favourite book, Charles Kingsley's *Alton Locke*, which, though it belonged to 'another age' (it was published in 1850), did show there could be hope for society. She sent him 'a little horrible cheap edition'. Pierre asked for more information about social reform and Margaret said he must read Canon Henry Scott Holland who started the 'Lux Mundi' group of modernist Christian reformers in London and Oxford. Pierre had got to know more about street-poverty and was curious about it, so he decided to go to one of the centres of European deprivation, London's East End, where there was experimentation with inventive types of social work in the so-called settlements in the slums for working-people and middle-class students. In October 1901 he went to live in London for the first time.

London was no great distance from the Courts' house near Ashford in Kent. It was just possible to bicycle all the way from the East End, or there was a train from Charing Cross on which he could take his bicycle to use at the other end to reach Kingsnorth from Ashford. Pierre was surprised that he was not immediately invited down, but was philosophical about it. The Courts had moved out of their big old house and were renovating a smaller one on their land. Violet wrote cheerfully to say he would soon be welcome and that Margaret could not write because she was brick-laying.

The story of the trio now enters darker times because its holiday period was over and the wasteland of the metropolis began to impinge on Pierre, and even on Margaret. Violet was away in Paris for much of the time with her painting. At first Pierre lodged in London with friends of the Courts, the Dales. (Mr Dale was later to play an incidental but crucial part in the story of Pierre and Margaret.) In *Two English Girls and the Continent* an interesting conversation takes place in their house, though there is no corroboration of it in Roché's papers. Whether or not the exchange actually occurred, it throws light on Pierre's relationship with the English girls. At a dinner-party Claude/Pierre is asked the polite question, why had he come to live in London? He tells Mr Dale it is to see the unusual girls he likes to call his sisters.

'But they are not so unusual,' said Mr Dale. 'I know numerous young women in London much the same as them, just as nice.'

(You would agree, wouldn't you, my sisters? I said to myself.)

'Honestly, why do you think they so extraordinary?'

'They are sincere, modest and they want to lead useful lives. They have energy, humour, personality and cultivation.'

'Good for them!' smiled Mr Dale. 'This is *English*, is it?'

Claude/Pierre asks Mr Dale if he believes in mixed marriages, between French and English people. Not really, he replies, though such marriages could work with intellectuals ('les penseurs et les artistes'). Mrs Dale remarks that she is very fond of Mme Roché, an honorary English woman. 'How would you class her?' she asks the son. Claude/Pierre replies elegantly and more profoundly than the Dales realise, in view of Mme Clara Roché's effect on his sexual destiny. 'I don't *class* her at all: I am part of her. When I was a boy, I wanted to marry her.'

Pierre became absorbed by London in the same way as Margaret had been absorbed by Paris. *Two English Girls and the Continent* portrays the city as a visually vivid, fragmentary, and sometimes surreal world. (Truffaut's film version does not: the whole of Pierre's and the girls' London experience is excluded.) There is one notable vignette. Pierre is travelling on an early morning London Underground train ('le tube à quatre sous') on to which clatter two dozen soldiers in khakis, with haversacks, rifles and pieces of kit attached to their uniforms. The sergeant in charge is a handsome ('chic') man who delivers laconic orders. He has a blonde working-girl with him, with bare pink feet, who must be his woman because she carries his rifle and leather dispatch-case. She does have shoes, polished to chestnut, but looped over her shoulders. (Why isn't she wearing them? Were they too tight? Had she and the sergeant left home and bed in a hurry?) There is a box of carrots next to her. Pierre christens her 'Albion', a better representative and fresher bloom of England than the stout Britannias of *Punch*. He watches her large hands on the rifle: a perfect conscription poster.

The 'love philter' is a traditional motif in stories of romantic love, the potion which infects the unwary. A foreign strain enters the system, or a strain of the foreign. 'Albion', the soldier's companion on the underground railway, epitomised London for Pierre: the sight was a Cupid's arrow which entered his bloodstream and prepared him for something new with Margaret, even though he doubted whether anyone could be 'the one'.

In London Pierre's 'official' mission was to go as a Socialist and investigator 'informateur' intending to see society and live close to poverty at Toynbee Hall in Whitechapel in the East End. There he joined a community of young men working in slum conditions, lodging in the Hall's spartan dormitory building, Balliol House, named after the Oxford college most involved in this work. Pierre joined Toynbee partly because of the influence upon it of the teachings of philosopher T. H. Green and the brilliant left-wing economist Arnold Toynbee. Toynbee was a Londoner who had done charity work in the East End under a reforming clergyman, the Reverend Samuel Barnett, vicar of St Jude's. In January 1883 he had given a controversial lecture about poverty which created a stir in London because it criticised Henry George's *Progress and Poverty* (1881). It ended with a powerful address and apology to the working-men of London.

> We, the middle classes (I mean not merely the very rich), we have neglected you; instead of justice we have offered you charity, and instead of sympathy we have offered you hard and unreal advice; but I think we are changing. If you would only believe it and trust us, I think that many of us would spend our lives in your service. You have – I say it clearly and advisedly – you have to forgive, for we have wronged you; we have sinned against you grievously – not knowing always, but still we have sinned and let us confess it; if you will forgive us – nay, whether you will forgive us or not – we will serve you, we will devote our lives to your service, and we cannot do more.

Toynbee voiced the guilt, the social conscience, and the determination for change that possessed many observers of the time, especially young ones. He was only thirty-one years old when he gave this lecture and already ill: six weeks later he died. He was commemorated in the name of the university settlement in Whitechapel which was established by Barnett and his wife Henrietta to initiate young people into the sense of service to the working class which Toynbee in words and actions exemplified. It was designed in Gothic style as if the residents would be Arthurian knights of social justice. This is where Pierre lived, taught, read and did errands in one of the worst slums in Europe. Like Toynbee, he was aware of poverty and capitalism, but unlike him Pierre was aware of contesting the exploitative system by becoming a different sort of person, one immune to and on guard against possessiveness and exploitation, performing a small-scale revolution in the self instead of trying to reform the world. The bohemian would be a long way from frivolity if his licence was a *non serviam* to capitalism.

In December 1901 the Courts thought their house was ready for visitors and after Christmas, on the first Saturday afternoon in January 1902, the trio resumed its life.

Pierre went down by train and bicycle to see the sisters. Margaret was gardening on a border by the house, in her plum-coloured bonnet and boy's boots. She was determined not to be impressed by Pierre's arrival so made herself finish digging a row. She was so self-conscious that she thought Pierre would hear her fork scrape the wall from inside the house. She made it scrape. Nothing happened, so she went down to feed the pigs. When Violet brought him out, she blushed as they shook hands. Violet definitely noticed. He was invited again and began to spend each weekend at Kingsnorth. He found the girls in an idyllic countryside environment. The Court property was nearly surrounded by a river with a water-mill. The Courts sometimes called it 'The Island'. Pierre gradually became aware of the realities of the household out of the holidays. Violet could be irritable: as a full-time art student she chafed at the chores she had to do for her mother and brother, thereby losing good light for painting. Margaret was distant, seeming to play again at avoidance of Pierre. He once sleeplessly wandered into the mist-wreathed garden at midnight to discover Margaret there and ready to tell him how much she wanted to talk, which put them back on their old course as friends. However, the midnight meeting was noticed by a maid who reported it to Mrs Court. Fortunately the maid thought she saw both sisters in the dark with Pierre, a relatively small offence, but even so, Mrs Court thought she must 'have a word' with Pierre because there had in any case been village gossip about the trio's noisy rambles into Ashford and the surrounding countryside. She called him in for a more-in-sorrow-than-in-anger interview, which Pierre actually found unexpectedly arousing. She told him she admired Mme Roché who had resolutely remained a widow, perhaps a strange reason for congratulation. She complimented Pierre on being a 'gentleman', using the English word. But she explained that she had to beware scandal and that he must take care to behave properly, even to set the girls an example. Pierre was excited to hear Mrs Court talk as if he were in pursuit of Margaret. She even hinted that were the involvement to become deeper, it would please her. She was surely implying he would be welcome as a suitor. It seemed as if reproof for late-night ramblings on 'The Island' was turning into a invitation to join the Court family.

It seems that Mrs Court dithered, or was 'silly stern' with Pierre. In him the apparent invitation lit a short dry fuse. He returned to London at full pelt. At Toynbee Hall he wrote immediately to Margaret. He told her that he *loved* her and that he would stay in England with her. They would marry, he said, but he made it clear that he must carry on with his efforts to know society, as 'informateur', not bound to the ordinary rules of marriage and monogamy. Margaret would be his wife and comrade, but he must have companions, even sexual companions. He was exhilarated by his own honesty. He was moving from love of two sisters (as he had assured Jo Jouanin) to the choice of Margaret and told her the truth. Mrs Court gave him the cue to tear Margaret, so to speak, out of their group photograph. 'The dogs were unleashed', wrote Henri Pierre Roché in his novel, a sentence used by Truffaut in the voice-over of his film with sinister insistence, like a line from Racine, redolent of tragedy. And something like tragedy ensued. The first phase in the story of the trio was over.

The letter in which Pierre declared his love to Margaret does not survive, nor did Roché write such a letter for the appropriate moment in *Two English Girls and the Continent*, in which Claude/Pierre's decision to declare himself is simply narrated. But in the novel we do have Margaret's reply. It appears like this.

> Your letter is terrible.
> You hardly know me.
> I love you as a sister, and not always that.
> Dispel your romantic vision.
> I love hardly anybody. I am clumsy.
> All I want is Anne [Violet] and my brother.

We know that Margaret wrote telling Pierre that she did not love him in *his* way, and she said so repeatedly in the weeks that followed. She questioned the bohemianism of his proposal, but as a serious person she did not reject it on account of its strangeness. She did not know what she felt.

> I do love you very much – tenderly, deeply, but not that kind of love – not 'like you', not 'am fond of you', but I love you, and I hardly love anyone in the world. But it is not the love you want.

It was now mid-January 1902. Violet was soon to return to Paris after her Christmas visit. Before she left, the three of them met in London and the trio was fanned temporarily into life, though with the difference that Pierre was now a suitor. For this period in the story of the trio we have to reply on Roché's novel – which may alter what really happened in one particular respect. We know that when Pierre first met Margaret he had talked to her about the freedom of French morals in general terms, and also about prostitution. But we cannot be sure that Violet was present at his most shocking revelations about prostitution. We know that Margaret thought her younger sister was still innocent of this knowledge (as will emerge a little later in the story), but it might have suited her to believe that she was the sole possessor of Pierre's worldliness. However, in Roché's novel, it is assumed that Anne/Violet knows as much about *filles publiques* as Margaret. Perhaps she did, or guessed enough.

According to *Two English Girls and the Continent*, the sisters still wanted to listen to their mentor, 'The Continent'. Walking around Bloomsbury, stopping in tea-rooms and parks, Pierre told them stories about his experiences during his months in the army, in Spain and in London before Christmas and his reunion with the sisters. In particular, they listened raptly to three of his stories about women.

The first story was about Thérèse, a circus performer who had migrated to Montparnasse from the provinces; the second was about a woman whom Pierre had met on a snowy night in Bloomsbury; and thirdly there was the story of Pilar whom he met in the cathedral at Burgos: but Pierre only said he had watched and followed her, not that she had seduced him. The trio returned to the piquant conversations they had enjoyed in Paris, in which Pierre had described how differently relations between men and women were managed in France, conversations which included his, to them, shockingly acquiescent ideas about *filles publiques* and prostitution in general. The sisters were now fascinated by Pierre's tales of independent women, women who had ceased to be girls, and had edged into female autonomy. They were particularly excited by the story of the woman Pierre met in Bloomsbury who is described in one of the most beautiful passages of *Two English Girls and the Continent*.

Midnight. On the streets, a covering of snow. I was walking past the grand entrance to the British Museum. Under a large branched street-lantern, a thin unmoving silhouette interested me. I approached. She did not move. I looked at her. A phantom? The Edgar Allan Poe's 'Leonora'? Watts's *Hope*? A Virgin ready for the Minotaur? Simple, dressed in black, carefully, new gloves of ordinary material. With great dark eyes, a little veil, and, it suddenly came to me, she was the little sister of the girl on the [tube]. We were alone. She roused herself and advanced one step towards me, stopped, seeming to hesitate. I took four paces forwards. I offered her my arm. She took it, modestly. And arm by arm, slipping on the snow, we made our way forward down the long wall of the British Museum.

'You look exhausted,' I said. 'What can I do for you?'

Silence, then, in a harsh voice which grated:

'*Nothing. Thank you.*'

'Where would you like to go?'

'Where you wish.'

A long silence.

'Where do you live? With your parents?'

No reply.

The little tongues of gas-light flickered; I had never seen *such* an English girl. She started to speak. Her voice became clearer, but her cockney accent was so thick that I could hardly understand her. We reached the wall along the second face of the Museum.

Take her home to talk? She would be shown the door by my landlady. A café? There was nothing near at this hour. There was a pub I knew well about a mile away, but where could I get a taxi? Perhaps a pub would be insulting to her. The policeman was back. Was he going to stop us? No, he wouldn't.

In *Two English Girls and the Continent* the reactions of the sisters to this tale typify their temperaments: 'Anne was pale, Muriel red.' Anne/Violet knows that Claude/Pierre has talked acquiescently about brothels in France and how they serve a good purpose: she says that even if they are evil places, at least in a brothel a girl is sure to be paid something. On the street she is despised, and risks attack. Anne/Violet asks what would have happened if Claude/Pierre had met the Bloomsbury girl in Paris. 'I would have been able to find her work. I could have introduced her to my mother.' The sisters are astonished. 'Just on the strength of this first impression?' they enquire and Claude/Pierre retorts that he would not have known *them* but for his first impression of Anne/Violet across the drawing-room at Arago. Muriel/Margaret wonders whether the girl has left home as a result of a family crisis. Was she in flight, for the Thames, perhaps, like Mirah in George Eliot's *Daniel Deronda*? In the imaginations of the sisters this girl becomes a special heroine. Anne/Violet says she would like to paint her, 'abandoned, but armed in her beauty' like Cophetua. She proposes they should call her 'Hope', after the woman in G. F. Watts's painting – though reproduction without colour makes the work look dimmer, more 'Victorian', more wistful than it really is.

It was this painting about which Pierre and Violet enthused together when they first met in Paris. It was 'my most favourite picture', Violet said then and Pierre knew it, too. It now became the trio's totem, as it was for many British people whose halls or parlours were decorated with reproductions of it. It had some of the popularity of Rodin's *The Kiss* in its solemnity, though the subject was very different, this massively moulded woman seated on a globe, in a silky garment evidently wrinkled by a cosmic breeze. She resembles a sketch for sculpture, like one of the Henry Moore drawings of war-time figures sleeping in Underground stations below London. The painting does not have the kinetic energy of a Rodin: it is obviously a *picture* of a bodily form. She is blindfolded, head lowered, her fingers on her lyre with the broken string. Seemingly she is 'Woman', perhaps waiting, but for what? Freedom? Recognition? For her lyre to be mended, so she can play again? In 1904 G. K. Chesterton wrote a short book about Watts containing some brilliant paragraphs about the painting. He remarked that its name is a puzzle. Is *Hope* the name of the woman or of the painting itself? He thought that Watts wanted to paint something inexplicable, and that the painting seemed to be made by two artists, both of whom 'felt a swift, violent, invisible thing in the world', but one said the word 'hope' and the other painted a picture in blue and green paint.

> The picture is inadequate; the word 'hope' is inadequate, but between them, like two angles in the calculation of a distance, they almost locate a mystery, a mystery that for hundreds of ages has been hunted by men and evaded them.

The mystery is a paradoxical quality, an amalgam of fragility and resilience. Watts 'perceives that the queerest and most delicate thing in us, the most fragile, the most fantastic, is in truth the backbone and indestructible'. Chesterton thought Watts was trying to convey unsentimentally something which was equally tough and vulnerable, like the paradox which the trio sensed in Pierre's snow-bound figure in Bloomsbury. This girl, now called 'Hope', was ranked with the other model figures described by Pierre, Thérèse and Pilar, all three of them resolute. And one of them was known at this stage to be 'bad' – at least Violet knew it because she surmised that this 'Hope' could be a prostitute who in France would have had protection in a brothel. Such badness was not yet understood by Margaret.

Violet returned to Paris, where she now was to lodge with Mme Roché, an arrangement which kept a line into the enemy camp open for Pierre's mother. Violet wrote encouragingly to Pierre who was bewildered as to whether Margaret wanted him, or could want him. Violet said that she herself would be devastated ('anéantie') if the gulf between her and a loved one felt unbridgeable – she may have meant between herself and Pierre – and that she would always reserve a pocket of hope. He had said to her that he had been reading in Nietzsche that value could be learned through suffering. Violet would have none of this and retorted that 'Suffering is death.' If he thought she could help, he had just to telegram, 'Come!'

Margaret now had fewer opportunities to see Pierre. While her sister was in England she could say that she was going out with Violet and then they could all meet up in London and be the trio again. Now it was difficult to get away. When she did, Pierre told her that he had finished with France and that he would soon be leaving for Paris to make the arrangements to move permanently to England. Margaret protested that a relationship would not work – despite this, and simply as a result of arguing together, she and Pierre were becoming a couple.

Pierre was settled in Toynbee Hall, working in Whitechapel, venturing out, but never alone, into the alleys that had once been terrorised by Jack the Ripper, teaching French to anyone who turned up at the settlement and living in its hostel, Balliol House, which was used for the workers, providing plainer digs than the accommodation in the Hall itself which most of the British students used. Ironically, he was the one who had mocked charitable 'slumming' in the Paris conversations; even now, with so much to say about themselves, Pierre and Margaret went on arguing about the ethics of 'going about the world doing good'. Pierre joined in all the Toynbee activities, including mock-debates in parliamentary style and boxing bouts, in which he promised not to use his feet. Margaret was curious about this life and would have loved to be a Toynbeeite. She once donned a white apron to help serve up sandwiches at an East End Sunday tea organised by the Hall. Pierre accompanied her back to the station, and on the way they picked over the Whitechapel street stalls for used clothing: Margaret could not understand a word that was being said. They had the excitements of lovers. On one occasion Pierre went to meet Margaret's train at Charing Cross but she didn't appear. Was he at the wrong station? Did Victoria serve the Kentish towns as well? Pierre hurried miserably out to Trafalgar Square where he saw Margaret in her long coat, on the steps of the National Gallery, smiling nervously down at his chagrin. They walked around the gallery. Margaret was unexpectedly upset by Rembrandt's portrait of his father and would not look at it. They had high tea in cheap A.B.C. restaurants, one of the few places in London where girls could respectably meet or wait for men. Pierre, lover of the Impressionists, remarked extravagantly that the brilliance of her redgold hair was like a split poached egg.

It seemed as if they were near a union, a couple with a future, but not for long. Trouble came first from Mme Roché who had always been afraid of the consequences of Pierre alone in London with Margaret. Then danger erupted, more frighteningly for Margaret, from Pierre himself.

Pierre had told his mother he wanted to marry Margaret and settle in England. So: her son wanted to marry a sickly, difficult and irritatingly *English* girl; her child bred in the womb for a love of art, according to the Roché family legend. On her own side Margaret assessed the situation dispassionately. She said that she realised Mme Roché thought that Pierre would be yoking himself to 'an irresponsible, hysterical daughter-in-law'.

Pierre returned to Paris early in February, quixotically believing his mother could be placated. Margaret was aware of the danger of antagonising her. 'Think of the *horror* of living with Mme Roché's hatred and misery forever hanging over you.' But the more she thought about the danger and the unsuitability of Pierre, who showed no signs of giving up his libertarian views, the more she thought about marriage. Strictly speaking she had rejected Pierre, but this only started a new phase in their friendship, with Margaret thinking about 'us' as if they were a nearly engaged couple with problems to surmount. As for Mrs Court she was nervously worrying whether Margaret was, as Mme Roché had harshly opined, physically unsuited for marriage, so an appointment was made with Dr Wilks, the family doctor. He concluded that Margaret was 'a rather slow-pulsed creature, with not very good circulation, but basically healthy and certainly could marry', a verdict which Margaret exuberantly retailed to Pierre by letter. When Dr Wilks was told that the

French mother of Margaret's suitor was obstructive, he just said, 'Well, I hope things will mend, but if in time the horses still look the same way, I should just harness them and drive off.' At that time the question of being healthy enough for marriage was seriously reckoned. A hundred years ago, when some diseases were ineradicable, 'fitness' was understood in a way now lost: it meant not merely being in good shape, vigorously healthy, but fit *for* something and suited to a *purpose*.

Mme Roché's opposition was tolerated by Margaret and almost relished because it placed her in the common thoroughfare or classic predicament of being a potential daughter-in-law opposed by a hostile mother: a refreshingly ordinary dilemma. The greater trouble that erupted – and a truer source of agony – derived from Pierre himself. When Margaret wrote to Pierre, made more cheerful after her interview with Dr Wilks, she told him that she was his ally or friend, ready 'to help, if not quite to love yet'. Pierre wanted more. As yet Margaret showed no sign of the sexual desire he longed to find in her. He was now feeling guilty over the stories he had told about Thérèse, Pilar and the British Museum girl they called 'Hope'. In each case he had movingly described these solitary, beautiful and courageous women who did not enjoy, or were stifled by, the bourgeois comforts of his British sisters. He had painted them as innocents abroad, like George du Maurier's Trilby. But he had not told the whole truth about his attraction to them. He had not said that *the* basis of the encounter in Burgos was erotic, a delirious mutuality into which he had been invited. Pilar was not a suffering heroine, but a freely sexual person. He was beginning to think that his part in life might be that of an enabler like her, doing for women what she had done for him: a liberator as well as a libertarian. Pierre realised that stories he had told in London were told in bad faith because he had evaded the cardinal fact of sex and the important idea of liberation. He therefore resolved that Margaret had to know the truth, as his comrade. He wrote to Margaret confessing that he had been to bed with Pilar.

A desire for honesty and even bluntness shone out of Pierre Roché from his earliest years. He hoped that the confession would make Margaret realise what he really was and wanted, perhaps even realise what and who she really was. He wanted to meet Margaret in the valley of sex and sensibility rather than on the high road of sense and conscience. He wanted her to know they were both implicated, like everyone else – intellectuals, suburbanites, workers, English and French – in the facts of sex, which is why he had implored her to read Zola's *Germinal*. The Courts and the Rochés could veil sex in sentiment and 'love', but Pierre, now reading Schopenhauer, was sceptical. He wanted Margaret to know that he and she belonged to the common lot, and that as 'Nuk' he unbearably wanted her. He told her again she *must* read the copy of *Germinal* she had bought in Paris.

For Margaret it was a terrible shock to learn that Pierre had loved Pilar 'in the physical sense' and broken the Sixth Commandment. Her first reaction was that her brother Stephen would fight Pierre: surely he and Mother would prefer her dead than marry such a man as Pierre. She did read *Germinal* and learned from it that she should be called a 'virgin'. She had semi-known this and semi-known about love 'in the physical sense', but she was now frightened of what Pierre seemed to be demanding. Did he want her to read Zola because of his depiction of social evil, knowledge of which belonged to their mutual sense that 'something must be done' about poverty, their undefined project, their 'task'? Did he want her to read *Germinal* so as to introduce the carnal into their friendship? Was his insistence on her reading it actually one stage in a process of seduction? Pierre had told her in Paris about prostitution, a new word to her then; now she remembered him asking something she had not then understood. Could a male virgin go to a prostitute and still marry a proper woman? 'If I had understood I would have said *No*,' she wrote to him.

When she first heard the story about the girl in Burgos, she thought Pilar was a young heroine. Now she became a woman wronged by her honorary brother, who was not even ashamed of what he had done, as her brother Stephen would have been. 'An Englishman honours a woman from the heart.' It was well and good to talk theory about the French way of life, about civically useful brothels and medical examinations. It was a different matter to know that Pierre had done what a decent English man would think disgusting. She now had to grasp what 'virgin' meant and 'The Thing'. She could not bring herself to write the words Pierre used. She wrote the initials 'S. R.' in her letters to stand for 'sexual relations'. On 22 February she wrote to Pierre in French.

> I suppose you think that I should be used to the idea, having read *The Lady of the Camellias* and *Les Misérables*, but actually one does not understand what one does not know. I did not know – in spite of the books – before *Germinal* taught me the fact. I was helped by *Germinal* and prepared by you [in Paris]. If a child has only seen butterflies she will not understand the word 'elephant', however often she sees it.

Adversity deepened the couple's complicity. Margaret was longing for Pierre to come back to London. She wrote anxiously several times to tell him what they had to discuss back at Kingsnorth (or in London), letters which show that a very English thing was happening: Margaret was beginning to cope. She still said she did 'not love' him, but she was writing as if they were an engaged couple facing up to a catastrophe she was determined they would overcome. On 3 March she wrote again in English.

> You love me tremendously – I only love you a little. Would it not be better, before I love you desperately, to kill the possibility of marriage, to separate for ever – utterly. We must talk about all this on Sunday. To think how much better for both of us, if you decide now, that you ought not to marry me than if you found it out later – after I had known or acknowledged my love. For I believe that if I love you as a man I shall love you utterly and for ever. If you decide now that it would be better for you and the rest to give each other up – why, at any rate, it is not outwardly too late as far as I am

concerned. If I found out afterwards that would be my own concern and need upset nobody. It is not too late.

Margaret then went over the reasons why they should probably not marry. There was religion: 'I still being a "Christian" in the exact doctrinal sense.' But she did use quotation marks around Christian. They had a social philosophy in common. But 'in a great measure the "realization", the "seeing" of the lives of others must depend on "feeling". You cannot have any correct, fair notion of a sphere of life outside your own without *feeling* that other sphere. Therefore you must live the life of that sphere for a time, in order to know it.' This was Pierre's mission, now confirmed by his expedition from Paris to Toynbee: *to know society*. Was 'feeling that other sphere' compatible with an ordinary family life? Wouldn't a home 'prevent or lessen this experience'? Margaret methodically set out and numbered the arguments.

1. If it were a sphere of misery, dejection, hopelessness which you wished to penetrate, the return, every evening or every week or few weeks, to my or your home might weaken the pungency of your experience – might even prevent your soul from feeling all the bitter hopelessness – all the horror you would, if you had no wife, have felt. To remedy this you might cut yourself off from 'home' for a considerable length of time and live a materially solitary life – for a year, or years even, but even so if *you* had a wife, you and she would be so 'one', your spiritual communion would be so real, her spiritual presence with you would be so evident, that you would not separate yourself from her. She would comfort you every evening – your head and your heart would 'rest' and refresh themselves in her. If all this would diminish your power – your work – you ought *not* to marry – even were your wife ideal.

2. It is possible that once married you should decide – on other considerations than your work – to have children. Once a husband is a *father* the interests and duties and joys belonging thereto might lead you away from the extreme limits of

work you formerly aimed at, might by taking some of your energies, make you incapable of the Work you now plan. If you should consider that humanity would lose by this you ought not to marry, *or* if you should decide that a wife would increase your power to work, then you ought to have only a wife and no children, I expect. And that decision, which would have to be mutual, and before marriage, could only come from an intensity, an all-sufficiency, almost an exclusiveness of passionate and deep love for you on the part of the girl which, just now, I can hardly imagine.

3. There is the possibility that your wife should prove a real check on your work. That she should prove mentally and orally incapable of accompanying you spiritually in your advance – incapable of the effort and fatigue and difficulty of climbing the mountain with you – of looking down, or standing with her hand in yours when you looked down the awful precipice, of leaping from rock to rock with you, over the chasm of possible failure. She must be capable not only through love of the *will* to go with you, but through constitution and training of the *power* to go with you, helping or hindering you. For this last case, it is not so much a matter of not marrying as of choosing your wife – of knowing her, trying her ruthlessly, proving her beforehand.

4. If the fact of having married would exclude you from those possibilities of an unmarried life which would be useful to your work, this would outweigh the advantages to your work, marriage – you ought not to marry.

If only they could talk. 'Oh, come soon, and let us try to find it all out: but we must try and judge all the base consequences that might follow our marriage.'

In Paris, Pierre saw Violet nearly every day. They could meet at Arago. She remained his 'sister', it seemed. Determined to be true to the principles of the trio, he now told her in a letter what had really happened with Pilar. Margaret had already written to tell Violet that Pierre had confessed a terrible secret, but she had forgiven him. Violet was prepared and was less startled by the

45

news than her sister. She left Pierre a note saying they must meet: until twenty-four hours before she would not have believed her 'brother' could have done such a black deed. She had no questions, but she had to see him because his personal presence would reassure her that he was still her friend Pierre. She proposed meeting at a café, or at a park bench that they favoured.

Meanwhile, Margaret was worrying about her younger sister. Now she knew more facts about sex and men from Pierre and *Germinal*, Violet should also be educated, she believed. She decided to enlist Pierre's help. She wrote to him saying she had written a long letter to Violet on the subject. She charged Pierre with the responsibility of helping Violet make the transition to knowledge. 'My introduction, weak and full of error, will lead Violet more smoothly, and with less shock, than you could have done. Now my part is finished – I can lead her no farther – you must do what you judge best. Don't go too fast. What I have tried to do above all has been to present facts as they would stand if all were natural and as it should be with no traditional evils or ideas of evil still clinging to them.' Margaret asked Pierre to go over her letter with Violet, telling her more than she could. Margaret's belief that she should educate Violet may seem a strange one. Here was a young woman determined to tell her sister about sex and have her near-fiancé participate. Moreover, as well as explaining the sexual relation or 'S. R.' 'as it should be', she wanted Pierre to go further and talk to Violet about the nature of prostitution. Although in his novel Roché shows Violet to have known about *filles publiques*, Margaret believed her sister was still an innocent. 'I have purposely avoided mentioning even the word "prostitution". I don't suppose Violet knows of its existence, but she may. (She has read *Les Misérables*, *Pendennis*, *Anna Karenina*.)' It was to be Pierre's business to explain the phenomenon. Margaret had gone over his old letters, especially one in which he wrote of the abuse of sex, of prostitution. How much she longed to talk to him, she wrote now, about how this social evil should be handled, even cured. 'What a glorious thing this would be!' We do not know whether

Pierre provided Violet with the education Margaret asked for, nor what Violet felt about Margaret's intervention.

It is not surprising that Margaret had prostitution on her mind, once she had made the shocking discoveries from Pierre and from *Germinal*. Her curiosity was aroused and curiosity about sex, in some phases of life, historical and personal, has to find its satisfaction in forbidden regions. If one wants knowledge of sexual behaviour, one wants specificity, knowledge of behaviour *some*where of *some* people. (And one wants the knowledge to be communicated excitingly.) When sexual behaviour is invisible, as it was in the world of Margaret and Violet, knowledge had to be sought in the deviant world: and the prostitute was a visible possessor and therefore a bearer of knowledge. No wonder she was an object of fascination. Sexual behaviour could not be successfully imagined by these sisters in a family in which the mother had no husband and the brother no girl-friends. When Margaret looked round at her female peers at other tables in an A.B.C. restaurant, she could not necessarily attribute sexual lives to them. The only certain place for unashamed carnality was in the world which was dedicated to it: the world of vice. Everyone was supposed to know about love. Everyone grew up, later or earlier, to know desire. But the place where desire was at this time indubitably canalised or channelled or manifest was only in the bad world. Pierre had talked to Margaret about prostitution when she first visited Paris. Now his theories had turned in her into an active concern. But this, the visceral interest, was not the reason that Violet had to be told. From Margaret's point of view – though limited, she had some experience of social deprivation, or 'Outcast London' and the ills created by the moral violence of industrial society – prostitution was a central economic issue, a function of an exploitative society. It related not merely to sexual identity, but was a major social fact, a knowledge of which fanned out to understanding of the structure of society. It could not be ignored by those, like the sisters, who laid claim to a whole and Christian view of society. (Today, by contrast, sexual knowledge can, probably, be deemed to reside only in the sphere of human relations. AIDS often is, and should be, part of a sex education programme, but as a health issue, not an issue with inherently political resonance, as was prostitution in Margaret's time.) Prostitution belonged, she believed fervently, with education in the 'facts of life'.

Pierre's stay in Paris lengthened interminably for Margaret, but at last in April 1902 he returned to London and went to see Margaret for four days. She was staying with her mother in a bleak cottage near Porthleven on the south coast of Cornwall. The pair of them walked up against the wind as the trio used to do. Margaret could not bring herself to say what she called 'the big yes'. She had been busy outside the home in Kingsnorth, coaching some school-girls, and had taken some nursing examinations. The shock of the Pilar story had faded, partly because she had thought up an analogy which helped her put it in perspective. She told herself that she and Pierre were like people who had been on a voyage of exploration and were carrying samples for analysis, like Charles Darwin on the *Beagle*. They were both 'informateurs', students of contemporary life which they should observe dispassionately. Margaret had finished *Germinal* and was thinking about parallels between it and Wagner's *Ring of the Nibelungs* which she had seen recently at Covent Garden. Pierre was still a determined suitor and remained obdurate in the face of Mme Roché's hostility to Margaret. It was beginning to look as if the situation could be weathered.

But opposition from Mme Roché intensified. At the beginning of May, Violet wrote to say that she believed if Pierre and Margaret married Mme Roché would never see them again, or their children if they had them. She was demanding that Pierre return home. He did so. Clara Roché now astutely avoided making commands. Instead, she reminisced. She told Pierre about his early life: how childbirth had been an agony for her; that it was days before she could hold him; how her sweet husband had laughed away her fears; how Pierre had been placed at her side in bed as she slept and how, eventually, when she woke, she embraced the infant instinctively and her fears evaporated. She described the death of Pierre's father and how ever after she saw Pierre as a memorial to him. By opening other doors for Pierre, to the past and to herself, she tried to expel the despised Margaret. Pierre said he had to go back to England.

The night before he left Pierre dreamed about himself at the age of sixteen, early in his sex life, creating an imaginary scene out of Gustav Klimt. His mother entered his bedroom, half-naked in an ornate costume. 'With the gestures of a priestess she lay beside me.' Then she opened his penis with a needle-like instrument, which she slipped inside to its full length, opening the passage like a finger in a glove. Pierre felt pain and his thighs wet with perspiration. The figure of Clara then vanished, but returned in even brighter ritual garments, and with a different needle pierced him deeply, but in a part of his body he could not locate. He woke with a tearing pain and the emission of sperm. Pierre said that after this dream Clara ceased to be a command-ing physical entity for him. He was still a son, he thought, but set free, to find another Clara. She would have to be the same as his mother, 'but also her opposite.' (Perhaps one of the sisters, or the sisters combined.)

He returned to Toynbee Hall in the middle of May 1902 and Mme Roché followed to stay with friends of the Courts near Ashford. She offered a show of temperate diplomacy: her proposal was that the two families should seek the advice of a third party, even though Margaret had not yet accepted Pierre's offer of marriage. The Courts' friend Mr Dale was charged to undertake an *arbitrage* to assist the widows. Pierre and Margaret were not to be present. He came up with the verdict of a one-year separation, in which the couple should have no contact, not even by letter. Mrs Court timidly suggested that they could decide about marriage one way or the other after the year was over, but the petition was rejected: marriage, said their friend, need not *necessarily* be discussed after the separation. Mrs Court took the news back to Margaret in Kingsnorth, still angry about Mme Roché's insinuations about Margaret's health, and would never trouble to see her again. When Pierre's mother told him the news he concluded laconically that she 'had won'. Margaret was stunned by a prohibition that seemed redolent of the Brothers Grimm, or of some dark fiction by Heinrich von Kleist. The courtship dissolved, but the trio was to prove more resilient than the elders supposed.

Chapter Two

will it be terrible,
or nothing at all?'

Down in Kingsnorth Violet was now home for Easter, so at least Margaret had someone to talk to. But she did not have much to say. For the moment she was a little relieved and separation even sounded adventurous. Her mother said it was only fair that the situation should be explained to Pierre in person, so she and Margaret visited Balliol House on Thursday 22 May 1902, to tell Pierre he could no longer visit Kingsnorth or see Margaret. But he was not at home. Mother and daughter left a note saying he could come down to Kingsnorth to talk about it. Pierre telegrammed that he would do so the following Tuesday. He arrived at Kingsnorth in cycling clothes so he could ride to Ashford railway station and leave a Court bicycle there the next day. He was supposed to catch the one o'clock train back to London.

This visit was momentous for everyone, but they were not to know how momentous: after it, Pierre and Margaret never met again in England. Mr Dale's verdict meant they could no longer write to one another, but they did keep copious diaries and notes. Margaret immediately started a journal in a blue exercise-book originally destined for school mathematics, labelled by her 'Euclid', and this was followed by a second similar book. These journals run from the parting in May up to November 1902 and then go on more sketchily to June 1903. Margaret also kept a journal later, beginning in January 1906, but between the summer of 1903 and the winter of 1906 it was hard for her to write because she was often ill and for some months her sight failed. She was for a time totally blind. In this third journal she can be seen to be recovering from mental and physical breakdown, but the early journals are initially idealistic and vigorous, with Margaret perpetually busy at Kingsnorth, the lonely bright one of the family, coping with her mother's fuss, her sister's silences, and her brother's material needs because everything seems to have stopped for Stephen when he came home to stay. These journals are selective and she wrote more than have survived: she kept another notebook, 'my pink diary', which is lost. In Roché's papers there are some loose pages from an exercise-book in Margaret's handwriting, marked up as material for *Two English Girls and the Continent* which were probably from this pink diary. Pierre also kept a journal about the separation in a Collins Golden Notebook, an exercise-book with a stiff shiny dark yellow cover. It is a cardinally important document in the life of Henri Pierre Roché which charts and evokes the first months of his separation from Margaret, months in which he decided on a lifetime project to which he remained curiously true in later years. This journal does tell us what he was doing, but it is predominantly a book of reflections, a record of decisions made, rather than a day-to-day diary.

Margaret began her separation by writing about what was happening in fictional form, casting the trauma of Pierre's parting into a story. It is a romantic account, leaving out the fact that Pierre was suffering badly at that time from hay fever. According to Margaret's tale, on this Tuesday evening in spring she and Pierre talked philosophically about the verdict, in the garden scented with gorse, and a smell of water coming up from the river banks. The next morning Pierre asked Margaret if she would sing at the piano. She had promised herself not to do so again, but did not have the heart to refuse him. She sang one ballad mechanically, after which she looked at him and asked him, softly and icily, 'Is that it?' He asked timidly for a Schubert song they liked. Violet, 'little loving sister', covered her face in her hands. A meal was laid out for Pierre in the garden. Mrs

Court, 'thin face thinner than ever', told Margaret to bring out rhubarb and cream. She said, 'Is there anything you wish me to say?' Margaret replied, 'Nothing, dear little mother, you have said and done as no other mother would and Pierre loves you.' (We do not have Pierre's thoughts on this.) Margaret threaded a daisy chain as Pierre finished his dessert and the practical Violet said he had better be careful not to miss the train. Margaret opened the gate and almost pushed him out, flicking the forget-me-nots that edged the path with her skirt. Pierre said *au revoir* to Mrs Court. It was Wednesday, 28 May 1902.

The sisters were due to play tennis at three o'clock. After Pierre left, Margaret took the medical text-books she was studying for her next nursing examinations to a deckchair in the garden and sat staring, elbows on knees and chin in hands, wondering whether she really minded: 'Will it be terrible, or nothing at all?'

Margaret's sugary account of the parting is interesting because it shows Pierre's diffidence ('sad, eager, timid voice') or at least that he was perceived to be diffident. Although Pierre became Henri Pierre Roché, 'the man who loved women', it should not be inferred with hindsight that he brimmed with confidence at this time and in this place – or that to be a 'man who loved women' implies the possession of confidence. He felt Margaret was dominant, showing this in references in his journal to the best-selling novel about bohemian life, George du Maurier's *Trilby* (1894), the theatre version of which he and Mme Roché went to see in the West End. They agreed that Trilby was rather like Margaret and that Pierre was like Little Billee, her adoring suitor, who is 'small' (in this unlike the lofty Pierre, though he was certainly 'slender') and possessed 'a quickness, a keenness, a delicacy of perception, in matters of form and colour.' Du Maurier's Billee is one of three inseparable art students in the Paris of artists and *ateliers*, and Trilby is the half-French, half-Irish girl, in a grey Army-surplus infantry trench-coat, with whom he falls in love. Like Trilby, Margaret had odd, bad French, 'not that of the Comédie Française, or that of the Faubourg St. Germain, nor yet that of the pavement. It was quaint and expressive, funny without being vulgar.' Trilby, like Margaret, had a beautiful neck of 'delicate priest-like whiteness' beneath her red hair. She was another 'Nuk'. Though Margaret was devout and unworldly, a country girl, she liked to say, she was also 'sprightly' like Trilby; perhaps too much so on the Wednesday morning when Pierre ate his condemned man's breakfast. Margaret was going to suffer badly, but she believed she could face the future. Soon after Pierre left she wrote that she was determined 'to fight down my melancholy'.

She knew that she would not see Pierre for a year, not until 28 May 1903. She did not have the company of Violet, who was restless, longing to be back in Paris, and soon left, so she decided to work, 'to go to slum for a few weeks', as Pierre had been doing. Margaret spent June and July making herself useful at two hostels for women in central and south London. She also worked in the East End as a rent-collector and fact-checker for the Charity Organisation Society. She was now in the world to which Pierre introduced her when she went to wait on tables at a Toynbee Hall meal for residents and locals. She was working from Newman Street in the area in which the Reverend Samuel Barnett had made his war on poverty. Barnett liked to say that 'the sense of sin is the starting-point of progress', something that was felt intensely by people of conscience in this period and is well described in the autobiography of a near-contemporary of Margaret, the Fabian socialist Beatrice Webb.

> The consciousness of sin was a collective or class consciousness; a growing uneasiness, amounting to conviction, that the industrial organization, which had yielded rent, interest and profits on a stupendous scale, had failed to provide a decent livelihood and tolerable conditions for the majority of inhabitants of Great Britain.

Like Margaret, Beatrice Webb worked for the Charity Organisation Society, a body which tried to balance its charity with strict organisation, making philanthropy systematic and 'scientific'. It provided funds for the poor but targeted the 'deserving poor' who could put charity money to best use. In order to establish the appropriate recipients the C.O.S. used a complicated form of assessment. The resources of families and individuals were scrutinised by the society's officers, many of them volunteers like Margaret. This was 'hard' charity and some people thought it callous and sanctimonious. The assessing visitor could all too easily humiliate or anger the visited. The inspector (usually female) was often afraid of her clients. Inspectors had to take meticulous notes on the actual conditions they found and were assessing, and in the preparation of these notes many of the society's aides learned to be practical social workers – and also writers. Margaret soon became one of the young women who had gained an education in writing as well as observation from the C.O.S., having joined the ranks of what were called 'trained investigators'. The exacting standards of observation were an education for many young people who learned them in the tenements and sweat-shops of an 'Outcast London' which was both terrible and newly accessible to the concerned middle class: the new Underground railways could take them from the Strand to the heart of misery in Aldgate and Whitechapel in fifteen minutes. The Underground stations were near the London over-ground railway termini which served the suburbs and rural areas, such as the Courts' Ashford. Young people, sometimes at university, joined social work enterprises related to charitable organisations, churches or other agencies, like the Salvation Army or the new 'ethical societies'.

Margaret's old school, St Swithun's in Winchester, sent girls to work in a settlement called Surrey Lodge in Kennington, south of the river, so Margaret stayed there for a while, then went north and east to St Jude's and Whitechapel in late June where the C.O.S. duty secretary explained that she could have a small case-load and instructed her in household visiting. Margaret accompanied an experienced inspector. She was given a reading list, at the top of which was *Homes of the London Poor: An Inquiry into the Conditions of the Abject Poor* by the founder of the C.O.S., Mrs Octavia Hill, which was followed by *Rich and Poor* by Helen Dendy, wife of the Idealist philosopher Bernard Bosanquet, an indefatigable lecturer on the issue of poverty.

'Each case is most complicated,' Margaret wrote in her journal. She was allowed to do follow-up visits for three cases, on which she had to take lengthy notes from the records at St Jude's, and given the usual work of a novice social investigator: the delivery of pensions to families in prison-like tenement buildings. She was frightened some of the time. There was one alarming woman, slovenly and about seventy with tangled hair, black dirty dress, and a sister ('hard-faced and bold') who hovered in the background in their stifling room. Margaret could not take her eyes off a cockroach on the sticky table. The sisters nagged her, insinuating that they should have more than nine shillings when their rent was three-and-sixpence (which Margaret mentally compared with the two-and-sixpence rent Mrs Court asked for the Kingsnorth cottages, where she was used to a gentler sort of visiting). In spite of the difficulties, she wanted more of this work: she realised she could do it and began to think about making a life in social work. Could she not train as a Poor Law Guardian? But a tangle of reasons kept her at home. Although she differed from Beatrice Webb in character, situation, talent and even eccentricity, she suffered the same predicaments: the underling status of 'a subordinate, carrying out directions, having to fit into the framework of family circumstance, studies and travels, friendships and flirtations.' Beatrice Webb had to take over the female duties when her mother died; Margaret had to support her widowed mother, to remain in waiting 'until Stephen or Violet marry'. Strictly speaking, Margaret as eldest was the first candidate for the altar, but she had convinced herself or been convinced that her duty was to look after the household, a sort of 'Wendy' (J. M. Barrie's *Peter Pan* was first performed the following year). Despite, or because of, her dutifulness she loved life away from Kingsnorth, living up in London with other girls. She started to understand a little of what it was like to be a working woman at Drury Lane Working Girls' Home. She realised how women could use cheap jewellery to brighten up clothes that could not be easily washed. Chocolate bars became important.

London was an emotional revelation for Margaret. The idealistic spirit in which she went to 'slum' is illustrated by the epigraphs she chose for the beginning of her journal. The first is a George Eliot-like quotation from Beaumont and Fletcher.

> Man is his own star; and the soul that can
> Render an honest and a perfect man
> Commands all light, all influence, all fate;
> Nothing to him falls early or too late,
> Our acts, our angels, are a good or ill,
> Our fatal shadows that walk by us still.

This is followed by a sentence of prose. She may have been translating something Pierre had written – 'The enlargement of social relations depends far less on opportunity, than on sympathy.' This was true of her London life. At home, looking after Mother, studying nursing and doing her errands, Margaret wrote from the heart with ever-turning convolutions. In London she lived and wrote from her senses. Within days she was inside a new life. 'I should not have thought only one week would have wrought the change in habit.' She loved the days off, when she went 'on amusement bound', one day to the Royal Academy by bus with her sandwiches, 'properly dressed in neat clothes, best hat and gloves'. Life at work was less inhibited than at home. On her last night at the hostel there were warm farewells. At bedtime, Lydia, who was usually undemonstrative, 'tucked her arm through mine and we trudged upstairs. Then still more to my astonishment she put her arms round me and kissed me so sweetly and strongly. Miriam, too, to whom I called 'Good night', came out and wanted a kiss, too, and I came up to bed with my heart just glowing, or something anyway, I don't know what it was, oh, I am so tired and want to lie down and sleep.'

Margaret was newly disciplined by the reporting procedures of the Charity Organisation Society and wrote up careful accounts of her London, like a description of street life and an 'elephant man' on Friday 27 June.

A crowd had formed, as if by magic, according to the wonderful way of growth of London street crowds, in its centre two tall policeman, handling something below them, hidden by the crowd. The policeman moved forward, the crowd parted and the object came to view, something on end, about four-and-a-half feet high, hung with exceedingly dirty brown stuff: rags. One policeman had hold of the thing by the upper end. The person – it – lurched to one side, a hand went up, and a cap was pulled off, revealing an awful head. It was the head of a man, but it is likely that a chimpanzee might have been less repulsive. The face was blotched up, red, dirty and pale and so horribly swollen and puffed that at first glance no feature was distinguishable except a blood-stained eye, the forehead cut and bleeding above. At the crown of the head was an enormous proboscis, covered, like the head but less freely, with bushy grey hair, the whitish colour of the skin showing through. The proboscis was a distinct formation, less in circumference than the head – and probably about one to two inches higher than the natural head would have been. The old wretched figure sunk into itself, the head between the shoulders slumped forward. The man was dead drunk. The policeman gently steadied him on his feet, pushed him forward and the crowd moved on. The old man rolled hopelessly, nearly fell, felt his injured eye and made but slow progress. After a moment or two a nice-looking lad with his sweetheart on his arm took hold of the old fellow's sleeve, and holding him at arm's length, followed by a few people, he led him along. He spoke to him in a kind, bantering way, and kept him as steady as possible, never leaving go for a moment. An elderly respectable man with white hair joined the three, walking on the side of the young girl. The old fellow put his hand constantly to his face. 'Leave that alone. Don't you keep feeling it,' said his guide, 'they'll soon see to that for you.' And so they moved patiently along the Bank Holiday pavement.

A new figure comes into the story, one who is surely Margaret in disguise, cast as a girl up from the country, which she was.

'Is the old man hurt, please? Are they taking him to a hospital?' asked a passer-by. She was a country girl and not used to such sights. 'Yes,' squeaked the old gentleman in so small a voice the girl had to lower her ear nearly to his lips. She had to give up trying to comprehend – with the sensation that a dwarf under the earth had been calling through the pavement. Her interest and pity were aroused, however, and she followed, slowly. At last the great hospital was reached, its closed iron gates passed, and the one open before them. The young man who had been talking a good deal to his charge stopped, and showed the poor wretch in with a smiling 'There you are.' The heap of rags and disease rolled out of sight into the shadow of the court. An exceedingly smart gentleman in a frock coat, fawn waistcoat and top hat came out as the drunkard rolled in, 'a doctor' supposed the young girl. 'That's right, straight ahead,' called the lad as a last direction and then he and his sweetheart strolled slowly on smiling and chatting and the country girl longed to go after him and give him a handshake and thank his goodness. She passed into the court but could see nothing but unconcerned officials. She caught sight of two children, peering through the next gate, and she ran, now knowing what they were looking at. There stood the terrible figure at the top of the steps, within the glass door. A tall official came up, and she saw, against the light from within, that he pointed to the hideous proboscis. Something was said, and a wheeled chair appeared, the old wreck, standing bent, knees bent, back bent, neck bent, fell in to the chair which cracked, and swiftly and mechanically he was pulled out of sight.

Alert though Margaret was to London life, Pierre was always on her mind. 'I generally have him in my thoughts if I am not actually thinking of him.' She overheard someone say the word psychology and suddenly saw lips puckering, pronouncing it in the French way, like Pierre – 'p-sychologie'. Was that Pierre, the tall thin man in the street under an umbrella? She dreamed about him several times. Once she dreamed she was in her bedroom with Violet, who receded into the background as a smiling Pierre filled her vision. He touched her side and bare back with his fingertips. She looked round and fixed his eyes, saying emphatically as sternly as she could, as if to a child, '*Je – ne – veux – pas*.' Then she kneeled to say her prayers. Pierre was sitting on the bed, she at his knees, both praying silently. 'But I sort of knew, from long habit of thought and dream, that you loved me, yet I had no feeling this time of our being lovers.'

She dreamed that she

had a beautiful little black ovary, I broke it in half, squeezed the seeds out on my left palm, and held it for Pierre to see the four beautiful cells. He took hold of the hand and looked at it closely a long time, then he said, 'But what – ever – can – ?' I knew he was going to say 'those lines mean?' And that he was looking at my fingers, not the seeds, and that he liked holding my hand. I felt mother's presence, and the 'separation' and that we ought not to be so [like this] together, and both of us simultaneously turned swiftly our faces a little towards each other, so that our lips nearly touched – and I woke, and we had said good-bye silently and got up. Vanished. The dream left no impress as before of happiness, just a sad 'fatal' feeling, quiet, though I have never before dreamt so nearly of kissing my brother, my brother Pierre (nor of any man, naturally).

Margaret must have been very determined to successfully persuade her mother to allow her to work in London. Social work was hard, physically and mentally, with all the visiting, teaching and maintaining relationships with many different types of people. There were administrators to be bossed by and there was the record-keeping, which was especially difficult for someone with bad sight. One wonders whether Mrs Court was aware of the risk of Margaret meeting Pierre accidentally on purpose because he was still at Toynbee Hall. Was she giving Margaret a chance to do so, to help them – or to spite Mme Roché?

Margaret hardly ever complained of illness, but she was

wondering about health in the context of what was better for Pierre in case they ever married, even though consciously she had never accepted him. 'Certainly it would be a life of constant requirement, and am I physically and nervously strong enough? Certainly I believe myself to be strong, healthy with excellent nerves – and yet *am* I fit? Morally and mentally fit?' She thought of taking up hockey again (she had excelled at the sport at St Swithun's). Margaret was not health-conscious in the modern way. Her idea of 'fitness' was transitive, *for* a purpose.

When she thought positively about Pierre, Margaret saw herself as if she were in partnership with a secular missionary worker, even a pagan or sociological one. The habit of such thinking was ingrained in a devout girl of her class, though usually related to a more conventional partnership, as a clergyman's wife, as indeed Margaret sometimes visualised herself. She thought about marrying a man 'who believes in a personal God, in prayer, in Christ's teaching as divine, a man who would work and let me help him among the poor.' In this mood, she 'looked coldly at Pierre in her mind's eye', saying to herself, 'Pierre, I can't love you', but 'then I smiled at him and loved him, my greatest friend, my brother'. She was sensitive to the attractions of the clergymen and social workers she met. There was a 'very clever accountant', who did the hostel's account-books and had a 'very uncommon head', beautiful slanting eyes, and the look of a Titian hero, 'always so gentle, soothing'. In her journal Margaret wrote down 'Miss Faithful' next to a little ink sketch of these eyes, referring either to a girl with similar eyes or to the fact that she was being Miss *Un*-Faithful to like a man when she was by now imagining herself (sometimes) to be Pierre's. She thought some of the clergymen were attracted to her. 'Once when I was in church, after the sermon, singing a hymn, the clergyman was looking round. I had just slipped into my coat and folded my scarf over my throat, my throat which gives so much pleasure! He looked steadily up into our pew in the gallery, and before a single thought, I had, while still singing the hymn, put up my left hand and opened my scarf, showing my throat and pretty silk blouse (the scarf *was* ugly).' And, 'instantly

I was so annoyed that I stopped singing and thought of Pierre and what he would say, and you might say, "it was instinctive, natural, not wrong". But I hope you would not say that, for it was wrong, wrong, *wrong*. I could say why, but I must stop.'

Pierre would certainly have said her attraction to the clergyman was natural. Margaret thought: 'I can't but have faith in Pierre, though I dislike and mistrust his theories, even deplore some of them.' How could she do otherwise? Pierre had told her that if they were together he would still need freedom of movement, a freedom that included sex with other women, though only occasionally did Margaret acknowledge to herself that this is what Pierre's theories involved. When she did face what he really meant, she still had to write down 'S. R.' instead of 'sexual relations'. Did he really mean he could 'have S. R. with other women besides his wife?' Was he 'going through a phase'? 'I can't have fixed views on his views till next year. He told me I must not till I had spoken to him. Another thing: he is young and passing through a phase which will evolve – perhaps acutely – in new directions. He will have different ideas in detail when he is older.' Margaret was psychologically suspended, sometimes crying to be snatched out of stasis. Sometimes, she wrote:

> I see things from your own point of view, judging from a third person's position – from Jouanin's for instance, and I say: if at the end of the year you still love that Margaret, her alone, and wish to marry her – ignore her letters, ignore her supposed feelings – go to her, at once, go yourself and simply flood her with your love, force her to feel it, its presence, its truth, force yourself upon her, force her eyes open – make her *feel, feel, feel*. She will then for the first time see you yourself as you stand in relation to herself. Give yourself full play, spare her nothing, do all that shall become a man and leave her then to judge at last for herself. Don't think of her suffering, don't restrain yourself for her sake. Let her suffer, let her fear – let her wonder. Go and fight for your love, go and do all that your truth and manliness approve – go, and win! That is what I would say were I Margaret your sister.

At the hostel Margaret could talk about subjects to which she had at first been unwillingly introduced by Pierre: girls and boys, 'followers', the dangers men brought to her ignorant charges because of the threat of pregnancy. She felt responsible because middle-class girls who knew about 'free love' did not set an example: church-going had declined and been replaced by the Sunday walk which could lead to trouble. Margaret realised that Pierre had taught her quite a lot about sex and society. She actually managed to bring up the subject of prostitution in one of the talks over cocoa with other workers. Like Pierre she now thought it central to the issue of poverty. But it was evident that the seniors, Miss Mowbray and Miss King, belonged to an earlier age, the Victorian age, and were hardly suited to talk, however timid, about sex and economics.

The Victorian age of Miss Mowbray and Miss King was soon literally to end, however: in the second week of August the coronation of the new monarch, Edward VII, took place. The event was also the end of Margaret's work in London. There were celebrations in Kingsnorth with which she *had to* help, as well as the harvest, and in the hay-making she was always supposed to enjoy playing a part. So she went back to the country and loss: she did not emerge from its tensions and 'my melancholy' for many months.

Meanwhile, Pierre was on his own and had no idea of Margaret's excitement at the thought of a life with him. When he had ridden away from the Courts' house in Kingsnorth, he had not looked back, according to Margaret's journal. She did not know he was calling out 'I love you' into the air. On returning to Balliol House he was so used to receiving mail from Margaret that he automatically checked his pigeon-hole. He had his new Collins Golden Notebook ready in which to start his 'Journal de Nôtre Séparation', marked 'Private'. He started by writing down the number of days they would be separated, and often wrote reducing numbers of days as time passed, but diary material was reserved for another notebook, a shorter one which hardly touches on 'our separation'. (There may have been other notebooks: it must not be assumed that all of Pierre's life was in the Collins Golden Notebook and the fragmentary diary. His more thorough journal – the *Carnets* – which he considered a life's work, was not started for another two years.) At tea-time, four-thirty in the afternoon on 28 May 1902, his basic concern was the brute fact of 365 days without Margaret with whom he was enchanted; he had meant it when he shouted that he loved her on the way back from Kingsnorth to Ashford station. He believed she did not really care for him and, now alone, he was more aware of impossibilities than possibilities. He listed four things that could happen.

Adieu
Amis
Incertitude
Mariage

On the third night back at Balliol House there was a dance, but its 'voluptuousness' was, he wrote, nothing compared to the sisters' singing of German songs on his last morning at Kingsnorth. In the following weeks he read Shakespeare, saw *Hamlet*, *Tristan and Isolde*, *The Flying Dutchman* and *The Valkyrie*. He liked the circular Reading Room of the British Museum, enjoying the leather-covered tables and ingenious brass book-rests, where he read Edward Carpenter's *Love's Coming of Age* about the paganisation of love and the poison of loveless, 'social' marriages. He found a translation of Jules de Gaultier's *From Kant to Nietzsche* (1900), a digest of philosophical trends that everyone was reading. At the time England was the home of progressive thinking, with the publication of, for example, Havelock Ellis's *The Psychology of Sex* (1897) and Patrick Geddes's *The Evolution of Sex* (1889). (Freud's *Three Essays on the Theory of Sexuality* did not appear until 1903.) He went to the public gallery of the House of Commons, which he curiously and revealingly thought was like Margaret in spirit; he thought his own personality resembled the Chambre de Deputés in Paris. He wondered briefly about marrying Margaret in church, an unlikely eventuality. He wrote down his pragmatic suspicions of the courtship formula: male pursuit, desire increased on capture, followed by its decline and the end of curiosity. And the prospect of children appeared absurd: 'We are two – we want to become one – we become three.' He speculated about romantic solutions. One was that at the end of twelve months, Margaret would say to him, 'Pierre, I love you. Good-bye.' Another was the thought of her dying in his arms. His favourite dream was of Margaret saying, 'Take me: we'll see what happens.' She did once say it – to her journal, and Pierre was not to know until years later.

He also thought and wrote about Violet, on pages with heavy ink deletions. He saw her as 'not-yet-woman', who could teach him things unlearnable from any other woman: states of mind and body that could be discovered or created with 'patience, care, intelligence and scientific method'. He imagined an erotic scene in which he spoke and guided an imaginary Violet who must have 'complete faith in me', communicating 'pure, worthy ("méritoires") things in sexual encounters as exact as experiments in chemistry. I would bind her eyes. It is necessary that she knows nothing of what I will say. This ignorance would be the base of the observation.' He would move forward by slow stages, pausing and ceasing at her least sign. It was love and sex as a sort of watching. Pierre thought of writing a story called 'The Model', probably a novella. He would have real models read it, perhaps help him revise it for publication. He wanted, he said, to elevate the conception of the model into 'something pure and useful'.

Amid the confusion and sexual frustration of life back in Balliol House, several things were surviving clearly from Pierre's experience of the trio of himself, Violet and Margaret. He was remembering how little Margaret and Violet knew about sex or about himself or about their own bodies, and how he had discovered that girl-boy relations were swiftly locked on to marriage, that outsiders had undue authority in the selection of partners and that the female partner was still a piece of property acquired by the male. He had discovered British respectability which he knew had an underside, the lower world which disgusted it (as Stephen Court would have been disgusted to hear of Pierre and Pilar in Burgos), a world in which 80,000 prostitutes in England earned a living providing sex so that women of virtue may be 'spared'. An invisible chain joined the women of virtue to women far away in the dark streets, such as the girl 'Hope' outside the British Museum. Margaret knew some of the same things, but hardly anything about the significance of sex. She was at this moment making reparation by work in the distant grimy rooms, trying at the same time to think less of Pierre and more of a decent English husband. As for Pierre, to him marriage was looking increasingly impossible.

On 15 June, after three weeks in suspension, Pierre re-wrote his menu of options by removing 'incertitude' from the list. 'Incertitude' meant, he decided, passivity, but now he wanted to use his will, a word which he appropriated from Nietzsche and Schopenhauer. If he had been dubious about marital happiness, he was now sceptical about the value of happiness itself, which suddenly appeared a trivial aim. At the opera he saw himself as a 'Flying Dutchman of the spirit' who had to explore suffering, at the risk of life and will. He now learned from a friend of the Courts that Margaret was slumming in London. He was less cruel about poor-relief work than he had been when she first visited Paris, having done it himself. He said to his journal that it was the duty of an intellectual to make a choice: one could do useful work for others or one could work for and on oneself, making personal inner changes that one day might affect others, even produce structural change in society. He wondered whether Margaret's job would bring her in touch with prostitutes. He did not make any effort to break the pledge against meeting; nor did Margaret, though she did not deliberately avoid Balliol House. It comes as no surprise to find Pierre returning home to Paris in the middle of July 1902.

In Paris his basic reading continued to be Nietzsche and a new writer, Charles Albert, whose recently published *Free Love* (L'Amour Libre) provided a lucid, Socialist exposition of the problems of love, sex and marriage. He told Margaret to buy a copy – or rather wrote down the publication details in his journal, which was destined for her eyes when communication was resumed. Albert made use of the progressive British writers about sex, Edward Carpenter and Patrick Geddes, and was one of those who saw the current relevance of Schopenhauer, whom Pierre had been commanding Margaret to read before the banishment. Schopenhauer brought new factors into the analysis of consciousness as well as into the analysis of society. It has often been said that Schopenhauer's 'will' (as in *The World as Will and Idea*) was an early nineteenth-century precursor of 'the unconscious' and stood in for some of the ideas contained in the concept later made available by Freud. His scepticism was in accord with the realism of the last decade of the nineteenth century and the first of the twentieth century. After Schopenhauer it was possible to believe that the controlling human forces were subliminal, and also sexual. Schopenhauer derided the collection of concepts and sentiments gathered under the heading of 'love', the vague idea that conveniently 'humanised', he said, the sexual instinct, the drive which he identified as a racial desire for the survival of species. It was just what Pierre wanted to hear. Preoccupied as he was with the here and now and becoming, and with multiplicity as a way of life, he wanted to do without 'marriage' and 'love'. Socialism taught him to reject the first in good conscience, and Schopenhauer explained the latter was a dubious quantity. Pierre was now liberated for the attractions of Paris. When François Truffaut filmed *Two English Girls and the Continent* he dealt with this moment in the story of the separation of Pierre and Margaret with a caustic geniality: Pierre meets a couple of cheerful and seductive Parisian women and his confusion evaporates. It is a reductive simplification: Truffaut gives no indication that Pierre was thinking and reading.

But progressive thought, as well as being critical of bourgeois ethics, also had constructive proposals. Charles Albert wrote in *L'Amour Libre* that 'for two people to bring to reality the physical and spiritual life of a new human being, that is surely the most serious contract that could be made! Does it not justify the most careful choice and *reciprocity* between those who make the contract, since between them is the most intimate union?' To understand the pre-eminence of sex, as one could from the recuperated Schopenhauer, was to acknowledge a prime factor in human reciprocity. The details which clicked, the erotic cues and clues which locked human beings on to their bonding courses, were given a new dignity. Margaret's neck, the *nuque* of 'Nuk', became important, not merely whimsical, not frivolously fetichistic, but an instinctive trigger to unanimity. Albert and Schopenhauer were validating the concept of sexual chemistry.

Pierre had talked to Margaret in England about what he called 'The Work' with which she sometimes thought she could help him, as a sort of secular clergy wife. He had clearer plans now: 'The Work' becomes capitalised in the diary. Some but not all of it was to be written in the form of an analytical history of Margaret and himself, a book which he felt was growing in him like a child. 'One never writes better than with the blood of one's heart. I will write our story, with shadows and strong lights. I will make a book of it. It interests me, first as our story, then as a work of art (if I am worthy of it), and thirdly as a *useful* work, about the non-intervention of third parties, and about love between different races and nations, and fourthly, as a way of educating young women, those who know nothing and ought to know more.' The book was not actually written until *Two English Girls and the Continent*, not, as Henri Pierre Roché was to write in red on his old diary, until '*52 years later!*'

One objective of 'The Work' was to make war on 'those who made ignorance of life and sex into a virtue'. Was it not shocking that Margaret could not read what others lived in *Germinal*? Pierre decided that in the analytical book he would anonymise the trio. He wanted Margaret to write a companion volume and to collect data for a second volume. She would be entrusted with the English translation and furnish an appendix of 'fragments' or case histories. They would be 'peaceful collaborators'. This never happened and in 1954 he wrote on the diary with his red biro that 'in the garden of our instincts we are going to gather what is necessary for healing'. The book was to be just one part of 'The Work', one item within his personal project, an ambitious, grandiose, life's work which included writing, but was not confined to literary or sociological composition. His work would be as much lived as written. 'I will study the moral, intellectual, social and sexual relations between Man and Woman.' Pierre's portentousness is tempered by an authentic Nietzscheanism when he claims he will express himself but adopt no posture or position, and accept no dogma. He will speak *in order to be contradicted* and will glory in the ideas which defeat him. 'I will write for people who do not have my ideas.' He will contest absolutes, and the generalisations of 'those who say that my badness *is* badness itself, or that my badness *is* "evil".' He declared war on the chaste person who spoke dogmatically against debauchery and on the *roué* who despised chastity.

Pierre began his researches in Paris and adapted once again the tested method which had proved so successful (and pleasant) before he went to England: advertising for contacts. He now had a philosophical motive, announcing himself in the press as a philosopher and socialist who wanted to meet other free spirits, and who was ready also to teach new ideas. He was now home in France, but he wanted contacts abroad. He had not come back to France simply to become a 'Parisian'. He described himself in his advertisement.

H. P. Roché (born 1879), graduate in law, former student at the École de Sciences Politiques, member of various international and humanist organisations, belongs to the '*modern* movement' in France in literature and art (as well as in philosophy, feminism, socialism), works currently in this movement in England, will be studying in Germany and in the United States on a project concerned with '*modern* psychology'; he wishes to begin communication with persons concerned with the same subject and to give lessons or papers in London, Paris, Berlin and Vienna. *Languages*: English, German, Latin, Esperanto.

Fewer replies arrived this time (about sixty). He wrote to, then interviewed, the better-sounding prospects from this 'harvest of human documents': the forty-year-old woman who had known Guy de Maupassant (she would be a 'friend') and two potential 'comrades'. He wanted all sorts, but especially wanted an 'equal woman' or 'sister spirit'. 'I will have friends, comrades, mistresses, but my soul will be my own.' He was not so keen on having an intellectual mistress who might 'weaken my mind' by the need to make himself comprehensible. There was one woman who might, in the right circumstances, be a 'mistress', a word which he self-consciously underlined. She was Germaine Bonnard, called 'Viève' by Roché, who was indeed to play that part in his life for many years, enduring his many other liaisons (including ones with Violet and Margaret).

At the beginning of August 1902 Pierre and Mme Roché took a holiday in Austria. On 26 August Pierre left her for mountain climbing on his own, staying at Rinn, a small town near Innsbruck. 'I want whatever happens,' he quoted from Nietzsche: and his menu of options was now halved:

Adieu
Amis

Mme Roché left the holiday early because she was not well. Pierre, however, was in a frenzy of good health, exalted by the clear air and by his new ideas, some of which were mundane ('Smoke only half a pipe a day') and some visionary.

Do not aspire to happiness, but to elevation.
Become hard: in the animal kingdom all the creatures are
  hard.
The aim is not to love woman or child, but to make a new life.

There would be 'The Work' with Margaret. (He had not asked her about it yet.) He was also going to create works of imagination which would be metaphysically sexual, 'psycho-coital' dramas. He would interest actors and talk with them about how some of this 'serious and fundamental project' could be performed. And the old haunting subject of prostitution recurred. He said to Violet and Margaret (but only within the pages of the Collins Golden Notebook), 'if you want to act, to *do something*, my sisters, concentrate on the prostitutes: there is the great suffering.' The trio had talked about the subject, but now, after saturation in Nietzsche and Albert, prostitution had become a burning issue for three reasons. First, the sight of the prostitute, on the margin of respectability, could visibly remind potential intellectuals like Violet and Margaret of the ills and contradictions within bourgeois society: the spectacle of prostitution called on the intellectual to be a free spirit. Second, prostitution displayed dramatically the dehumanising force of capitalism. There may have been, in the ancient world, 'civilised' prostitutes (*heterae*) who provided conversation, sex and society for men, but what was known about these women only served to heighten one's sense of the difference between ancient Greece and the industrialised sexual worlds of northern Europe in the twentieth century. Third, the prostitute was carnality made visible; the embodiment of those elements masked by verbiage ('desire', 'love') in the respectable world. The sight of the prostitute was an affronting fact of life. (That it was sometimes harder to identify a prostitute by appearance in England made the model all the more interesting and provoking: if a woman was mistaken for a prostitute she could believe, to pleasing or shocking effect, that she possessed an unofficial sexual viability.)

On the figure of the prostitute were focused theories of appearance and of power, theories that were the testing-ground for the new sort of life Pierre wanted. He liked to repeat after Nietzsche's Zarathustra that 'God is dead' and understood the slogan properly, that it meant not that there was no God (long admitted by many), but that 'Godlessness' meant that behaviour *must* change accordingly, an inference that was often not recognised, even by atheists. The slogan was used, but people continued to behave as of old. To live differently was 'The Work' for Pierre, in order to accomplish his personal 'transvaluation of all values'. He wanted to be a Nietzschean free spirit, but also, at the age of twenty-three and back in Paris, to be simply free in all the ordinary senses.

By the autumn of 1902 Pierre had an unparalleled opportunity for freedom. Mme Roché bought him a tiny apartment in a new block of flats in Montparnasse at 45 Rue d'Alésia, probably to assist in the dislodgement of Margaret. There Pierre could cook, write, talk till three in the morning with Jo Jouanin, and it was a place where both could meet their new women, the headquarters for a newly planned life and 'The Work'.

Just after moving to the flat there was a terrible dislocation of all plans. On 20 October Jo Jouanin fell ill with typhoid, and he was dead within three days. This happened exactly at the point when Pierre was ready to tell Margaret that the year's suspension would not work. He asked his mother for permission to communicate with Margaret to say they could only be 'amis', which seems a curious step and Mme Roché herself thought it so. Why say anything? she asked. But Pierre was exact: if communication was forbidden, then so was communication about non-communication. This punctilio was rather typical of his love of precision. He then chose the worst way to tell Margaret, an action (one hopes) attributable to grief at the death of Jo. A week after Jo's death, Pierre and Jo would have been going to the Concert Rouge. Pierre went anyway, and there met Violet who said she was returning home to Kent in a few days. He told her about his decision and the next day sent round the Collins Golden Notebook to her attic, asking her to take it to Margaret. It would explain everything. 'Become hard: in the animal kingdom, all the creatures are hard,' Pierre had written in Austria, inspired by Nietzsche. He was certainly giving Margaret something to be hard about in mid-October 1902.

Violet delivered the journal to Margaret. Margaret's reaction was to start another journal of her own, defiantly and with a purpose that was fortified by her experience as a Charity Organisation Society investigator and by the influence of Pierre and his idea of 'The Work', the desire to know and report. On the first page of the new diary she wrote that some people make fun of those who keep diaries. She may have meant her brother Stephen or one of her favourite teachers at St Swithun's, or Violet, though this is unlikely because Violet was to be the destined recipient of the diary in the case of her own death. She stated that she was keeping a journal

> on the chance of its being some day useful to Pierre or to myself, as a basis of dry facts, scientifically and accurately chronicled as far as I can, on which to build whatever structure he may think good to build. I will try and chronicle all that I feel might serve a useful purpose for Pierre and me. This journal will be for my eyes alone. If, during my life, I hand over the experience to Pierre, it will have to be cut and arranged (still keeping to Truth) for him. I would not write with the same absolute freedom unless I knew this was for myself alone. If I die before I give this to Pierre, then you, Violet, may give the whole to him, without first reading it yourself. There will probably be no need for this at present. It *may* be so, and therefore I say, when you have got thus far, stop and send the whole to Pierre. I want him to have all my letters and pages, whatever written since I knew him. Most will be only useful for the waste-paper basket, but among them he may find useful isolated bits. I trust him to use all his material for ultimate good. Let him never shrink from using me, dead, as I am willing he should use me living: roughly, coldly, cruelly. Anyhow, it is for the ultimate good.

When he first proposed to and wanted Margaret at almost any price, Pierre had said he would stay and work in England, but soon it was clear to her that he envisaged an open, investigative life. Margaret had tried to make the mental leap into Pierre's world when she was able to see him and correspond, but now it was too late. The month of July (about six weeks into the separation) saw the evaporation of Pierre's idea of Margaret as lover or worker-bride, even though he still and intensely wanted her as close companion involved in 'The Work'. (In his new post-Nietzschean state no-one could be clos*est* companion.) Margaret knew this when she read the Collins Golden Notebook, knew that Pierre was offering her less than before, however impossible his proposal of marriage had been. It is painful today to read her asking him to use her 'roughly, coldly, cruelly', let alone subjecting herself to his ideas when it seemed he had so little use for her: it is hard to be sympathetic to his demands made thirty-three years after J. S. Mill's *The Subjection of Women*. While it is painful to read Margaret offering herself to be *commanded* by Pierre, she is surely not to be pitied. Although she could not accept Pierre, she could, some of the time, understand his 'cause', the mission into which he wanted to enlist her. She recognised that it was a noble if strange cause, and one for which, at a deep level, a humbled sense of commitment was appropriate, the commitment which also exists in love. Pierre was 'unsuitable' in all sorts of ways, but Margaret took him seriously: he had, after all, chosen her for the rôle of partner-collaborator and she was ready to throw herself into it as she would have thrown herself into playing, indeed, being, the equivalent part in a match with a more comprehensible, a modern missionary lover, such as, say, Robert Elsmere, the best model of an enlightened clergyman, depicted in Mrs Mary Ward's famous novel, *Robert Elsmere*, set in precisely the East End London of poverty and charity that Margaret and Pierre knew. She wanted to serve, to be of use, and to be 'fit' to serve. She transferred to Pierre and his cause the emotions so familiar to her in her own church life. In church she had sung:

> Take my intellect, and use
> Every power as Thou shalt choose.
> Take my will, and make it Thine;
> It shall be no longer mine.

and:

> Just as I am – Thy love unknown
> Has broken every barrier down –
> Now to be Thine, yea, Thine alone,
> O Lamb of God, I come!

She was following the Nietzschean Pierre. But such following was not a Nietzschean thing to do: the *re*-education of followers was what Pierre wanted.

By sending the journal Pierre considered that he was saying good-bye to the period of suspension, but not good-bye to Margaret. He started writing to her again, in the Hamlet vein, as if to Ophelia. One letter returned to their old theme, the uselessness of charitable work with the poor. It only did something *to* people, when the age needed intellectuals to be *with* people or to *become* different people.

> To do charitable work, that's good, but what we really lack at present are people who will go down into the roots of social conditions to see and understand, rather than respond straight away to immediate needs. We need to understand the mechanism of the will among poor people, the structure of their minds and those of all the disadvantaged. We should not be giving, but making ourselves poor and into workmen, to work within the systems, as some of the intellectual Russian aristocrats have done.

Margaret was bewildered. She was willing to 'become poor' and took some steps towards it: she thought of trying to live for a time as a working-girl, using only her wages. But what was wrong with other sorts of aid, giving and helping? Surely it must be of *some* use to work as she had with London girls, even though it would not change her place in society (or theirs)? 'I wonder if Pierre knows it is far harder to drudge on at little quiet things than to plunge into heroic terrible things, but I *want* to do the big ones.'

One postcard said he had a mistress and Margaret wrote in her journal that the horrible abbreviated phrase, 'J'ai maîtresse', repeated 'itself mournfully and hopelessly in my ears'. She reprised it often, though unable to write down the key word: 'Still with his —?'

In the middle of December there was some relief. A sweet letter came from Pierre, 'affectionate, caressing, in sadness'.

Up to now there had been no plans, only misery, as she wrote her in diary: the endless strain of 'showing as little as possible to Mother'. Once, she said, she was 'not bright' with Mother. It was Margaret's usual fate to be too bright. Violet came home for Christmas and in one of their talks said that Margaret took the initiative too often; she should leave people alone: she was hyper-alert and 'interfered'. Violet did not talk much about Pierre, whom she saw occasionally in Paris, and Margaret pretended that Violet did not know what she had been through and believed – correctly – that Violet had not read the Collins Golden Notebook. Margaret did think about Violet being in Paris with her 'brother'. In her journal she declares: 'Oh, Violet I can't explain to you, but I can *write* it here. Don't you both see that if Pierre and you should love and need each other and marry in a few years, it would be far, far better that you should not know I love Pierre, that if you knew you could hardly accept as I could hardly offer my friendship.' She longed to tell Violet about what she had felt, to sob on her shoulder.

Margaret set a plan for herself. By the time of Pierre's next birthday on 28 May, she decided, the business of Pierre must have come to an end. But in January 1903, something happened which threw her into worse confusion. She went to London for ten days, once more residing in the working women's hostel in the Strand, in order to get advice about whether she could 'disappear' by becoming a working-girl, if only for a short time, perhaps three weeks to start with. Margaret loved the London that energised her. Her hostel address, though short-lived for her, was firmly written at the top of a diary page and she burst out with an emotion new in her relationship with Pierre: indignation. She noticed in the Collins Golden Notebook that in Paris Pierre had seen a play by Ibsen called *Love's Comedy*. It is a youthful work, written in 1862 when Ibsen was thirty-four, and it differs from his problem dramas of the turn of the century and the later poetic dramas. It is in a sprightly verse that translates well into English couplets, and is an unusually cheerful work, but one with a point that Margaret did not find at all amusing. It performs arabesques about the problems of love, marriage and commitment. Not surprisingly, Pierre enjoyed it because its thesis is that the main protagonists, Falk and Swanhild, should never marry *because* they love each other so much. The play had not been performed in England, but was translated and Pierre said to his diary that he wished Margaret would read it, and she did. Margaret was shocked by the play and in her journal turned violently on Pierre and his (and Ibsen's) clever theories. Did he think love could be turned on and off, or that the starting and stopping of love could be synchronised by will-power?

So you really think, you *really* think, that two people love or they do not, they come together or they do not, always mutually? Falk and Swanhild were very fortunate in agreeing mutually to part, exceedingly fortunate . . . What do you think I am? What do you think of me now, I wonder? Now? Do you think your change, carried on in dark and silence, doubling back on the former direction shown to me, do you think that change communicated itself, in the making, to *me*, and that I loved you less and less instead of more and more as I had loved and as I told you I must go on loving if I did not check myself?

What if I come to Paris?

What if I go to you?

Why? Why not? No – never – for it would lose you.

Do you not *see* that I am ready to marry you, *marry* you and leave you free, only spend the holidays with you, never have children, or having them to tend them solely without worrying you.

Thank God – yes, I say thank *God* – London is *drowning* it – and though it can never, I fear, kill it. I do begin to see the possibility of working, of working with enthusiasm, with *use* – with love – yes, *love*. Crushed by love for a man who doesn't want me? I *will not* so destroy God's purpose, I am a soul, a machine for work, I must do my duty, my duty to the world and my family, in time I may even say, I must cease to love Pierre and say already (though not with conviction) I cannot cease to think and dream of a time with Pierre. *Love's Comedy* is *false*. How bitter it was to read, and what a bad relapse it gave me, but already I am ten miles and whole miles onwards from anything I was or could have been or become. *Oh, if I were to live in London*!

Pierre, Pierre! I love you, I love you, I love you, Pierre.

Many years later, when Pierre had become the adult and elderly Henri Pierre Roché, after he had written *Jules and Jim*, he was asked what his next novel would be like. 'Like *Jules and Jim*, but with more *virtue* in it,' he said. Roché was interested in language and knew that 'virtue' did not mean the same as 'goodness' or avoidance of vice, but was associated with passion and valour, qualities shown by Margaret in this entry in her journal, and which Roché wanted to dramatise in *Two English Girls and the Continent*. When Pierre eventually read her journal he realised that her commitment to him was much stronger than he had surmised. Near this passage about her love, he wrote carefully in the margin in English (rare in these annotations), 'You have hidden it so well', and, in French, 'She never told me: I *never* knew it.' The tiny annotations in red, made in 1922, long before he began to make a novel from their private writings, do show currents of remorse at his leaving Margaret, but also bitterness that she 'hid it so well'. When he did plan the novel, he wrote on the inside cover of this exercise-book in which Margaret kept her diary that she tried to '*abolish* him utterly'. How wrong he had been.

For Margaret the abolition of Pierre did not work and she descended into a terrible blackness – but not until after a strange last twist which, although some months after Pierre left, was the last act in the drama of suspension. Margaret started 1903 intending to have done with 'Pierre thoughts' by the end of May, somewhat inspired by her reaction to *Love's Comedy*. When Violet came back to England for the Easter holiday, Margaret acted. She answered and capped Pierre's confession in his Collins Golden Notebook with a confession of her own. In her journal Margaret says that she wrote 'The Confession' which she then showed to her sister. Violet was due to leave for Paris the day before Pierre's birthday on 28 May – she was charged to deliver the confession to him.

> Violet left today – now, 10 p.m. She is driving through Paris. The night before last I gave her – she *read* The Confession I had written the day before, of that terrible fault the name, nature and gravity of which I only discovered, by chance a few days before, at the Museum. Here I will say nothing, all is written there, for Violet and Pierre.

Precisely what Margaret said in 'The Confession' we cannot tell. The material it contains is not in Margaret's journal, in which she simply says she wrote and dispatched it, with an interesting lack of anguish, considering (as we shall see) its contents, nor is there, understandably, any copy of it in Margaret's papers, or those of them surviving in the Roché collection, nor is there a copy among Violet's letters in the same place, though there are some references to its content. Roché's notes for *Two English Girls and the Continent* contain a scrap of paper saying he destroyed it at her request, and we do not have the request.

So for this episode in the story of Margaret Court we have to rely on *Two English Girls and the Continent* whose Chapter XIII is called 'Confession de Muriel' and begins, after the date 20 June, 'A bomb has exploded in my life, overthrowing everything. I have made an account of it for Anne and Claude: no-one else in the world.' There follow seven-and-a-half pages 'Written from 18th to 24th June 1903. The Irreparable'. (The date is a little later than the reference to the confession in Margaret's journal.)

It is not likely that Roché invented the material for this chapter. There are corroborative references, though without embellishment, to the central fact of the confession elsewhere in the letters of Margaret and Violet, and Roché in his notes shows knowledge of what she discovered 'at the Museum' which he is very unlikely to have discovered 'at the Museum' for himself.

There are three strands in Margaret's confession as we have it in Chapter XIII of *Two English Girls and the Continent*. Margaret (1) reveals what she found 'at the Museum' – that is, an American book, which still exists in the collection of the British Museum (now housed in the British Library), called *What a Young Woman Should Know*, which described powerfully how girls should resist being tempted to masturbate, (2) tells the story of how masturbation, 'Solitary Vice', had become habitual to her, without knowing its dangers, and (3) gives the text of a letter from an American organisation, the League of Christian Women of America: Purity Section, to which she had distraughtly written after she made her discovery. This letter congratulates Margaret for her courage and frankness. It urges her not to give up her fight with the bad, sensual habit. Of the three strands the last, the letter from the League of Christian Women, with its letterhead in Gothic type, is the one most likely to have been fabricated by Roché. (It is the strand used most powerfully in Truffaut's film.)* According to Muriel/Margaret the discovery of the book is bound up with the discovery of her own 'vice', but it may not have been the cause for this effect. Whatever happened, Margaret decided to make a confession of her own sexuality which complemented that of Pierre about Pilar. Using Roché's Chapter XIII and knowledge of the discovered book, what happened to Margaret is as follows.

Margaret had occasionally travelled to Bloomsbury to read at the British Museum, as Pierre had done; like him, she studied with a view to doing more social work. She had given some sex education to the hostel girls so she put in a call-slip for a book which looked useful: this was *What a Young Woman Should Know* by Mary Wood Allen and Sylvanus Stall, published by the Vir Publishing Company of Philadelphia in 1899. The chapter that most arrested the attention of Margaret was called 'Solitary Vice', about the pleasure girls can take in exciting themselves by touch, pleasure that she herself

* See Chapter Five, p. 188.

had experienced. Margaret now learned for the first time, or at least read, about it *as a subject*. Allen and Stall do not actually use the word. They warn that such pleasure can irreparably damage the mind and stunt development, a shocking discovery for one as steeped in Darwin and writers about evolution as Margaret. The authors demonstrate that pleasure in touching the sex organs can diminish powers of memory, drain muscular strength, cause types of insanity, all of which pathologies can even 'be transmitted to one's children'. They specify embarrassing symptoms, like blotched complexion and dull-looking eyes. (Roché uses some of these phrases in notes for his novel, which suggests he took them from 'The Confession' itself.)

What a Young Woman Should Know is indeed a powerful book that paid a surprising amount of attention to 'Solitary Vice' in women, a subject about which not much is confided a hundred years later and the prevalence of which was not in Margaret's time well known. Even in the late twentieth century it is agreed that women masturbate less than men. In 1993 an American study addressed the finding of Kinsey in 1948 that young men masturbate more than young women and decided, after a survey of college students, that this was still the case 'in spite of the efforts in the past quarter century to encourage women in our society to take greater responsibility for their own bodies and their own sexuality and to engage in more sexual self-exploration and self-stimulation.' The 1993 survey found that 81 per cent of male college students had masturbated, while only 45 per cent of female students had done. It seems unlikely that enough women masturbated in America in 1899 to justify a whole chapter on a subject which could have occupied part of a chapter on hygiene or health in general. It is true that the health risk of masturbation in women was higher than in the case of men – or such was the view of Allen and Stall, who thought that if women were careless about washing there was danger of genital infection ('pin-worms in the rectum' could 'wander into the vagina'). The authors were especially sensitive to the possibilities of infection during menstruation.

How the lining of the womb is restored is described with rapture.

> When the time comes, all the lining gets red and raw and the skin comes away in tiny bits. The many blood vessels all over the surface of the inner part of the womb bring blood which oozes out until the blood-boats have brought enough of the right building materials to make an entirely new drapery or lining. Blood, good blood, is needed everywhere! Once in every twenty-eight days the blood-boats have a great deal of extra work to do, and you must, like every good housekeeper, show some consideration for the little servants in your body.

The vividness or 'poetry' of this typical passage is a clue to the surprising prominence given to masturbation: it may not have been prevalent, but the subject was a pretext, a cue, for introducing a traditional theme of the delicacy of women, their special nature, a theme which helped corral and control them. The chapter is therefore a barbed attack on narcissism, part of a broad-based propaganda against bodily pleasure which can be autonomously created physically (tight clothing – very tight in this period) and psychologically (daydreaming about men). The authors wage war on pleasure claiming that the pleasure of sex which goes with the 'continuation of the species' is an 'exhausting' pleasure which creates lassitude. Allen and Stall are thus undeniably repressive and of course opposed to women 'engaging in more sexual self-exploration and self-stimulation' – unlike the authors of the 1993 American survey who were disappointed to find so little masturbation among women. On the other hand, it is possible to give some credit to Allen and Stall. The modern belief that women should 'take greater responsibility for their own bodies' is one curiously shared by Allen and Stall, remote and retrograde though in some ways they are. They may have derided sexual pleasure, which was, after all, hazardous in the monogamic world which Pierre despised but they did want their female readers to know pleasure, like 'sense of hearing in the study of different qualities of sound, tone, pitch, intensity, duration, timbre', and the recommendation of subtle pleasure was a mode, quaint though it seems, of urging bodily responsibility on young women. They disapproved of emotionality, or 'irresponsible girlishness', in their chapter on 'Friendship with Girls', and wanted women to be sober – which meant, not surprisingly, more like men. 'Two young men who are friends do not lop [sic] on each other, and kiss and gush.' ('Lopping' sounds indeed horrible.) They were repressive, but they earnestly wanted autonomy for women, an attraction for Margaret. But her loneliness in Kingsnorth with Mother made her vulnerable to the flesh-creeping and superstitious aspect of *What a Young Woman Should Know*.

The book horrified Margaret and 'The Confession' it provoked was a strange gift for her sister and her former suitor. Once again, as when Margaret entrusted some of Violet's sex education to Pierre, her determination to tell all to her sister may seem curious. But one should not underestimate the strength of the unafraid candour of young 'new women' (or potential ones) in 1903.

Margaret confessed she had known 'Solitary Vice'. It all began, she wrote, when she was eight and a nine-year-old school friend, Clarisse, had come to stay with the Courts. There was not enough room, so she shared Margaret's bed. Clarisse was a beautiful little girl, good at everything and a model for Margaret, curly-headed, 'with the air of an angel'. The children hid under their eiderdown, took off their night-dresses and played, one sure of herself and the other happy to be led. Clarisse, 'little pink sugar doll', showed Margaret it was nice to touch delicate parts of the body: nose, eyes, ears and just inside her sex. Margaret continued to see Clarisse until she was eleven, after which she went on pleasing herself, thinking it was all right so long as she did not really touch inside her body, though none the less she was awkwardly ashamed of what she was doing. Sometimes it was forgotten, sometimes it happened four times a night, and then it faded away in her early teenage years. At the age of seventeen, she told Pierre, it started again when once she was lying out in the sun with poppies gently swaying and butterflies darting around her, and she was flooded by desire. She wrote sometimes to a cousin saying that she did wrong things, promising to put a special mark on the letter whenever it happened. She did not specify what these wrong things were: her cousin thought Margaret was referring to loss of her temper. Sometimes there would be several code-marks on a letter. The 'Thing' (her word for sex after reading *Germinal*) went on, but faded after meeting Pierre. No-one had told her about sex before her conversations with Pierre. When he said that he had been touched by Pilar, she wondered if it was the same thing as with Clarisse. Had this been what Pierre called a 'relation spéciale'?

Margaret had known what she was doing and that it was not quite right, but having read *What a Young Woman Should Know*, she was appalled. Pleasure was now linked to sexuality, just as the word 'virgin' had been given meaning after reading Zola. For the second time Margaret experienced the difference between 'knowing about' and 'knowing'. In her head, her marriage problem with Pierre was at a stroke solved, erased from her agenda. He had gone and she must now not even imagine a reunion because marriage was forbidden to one who was not 'une fille intacte'. Was it this badness, this illness, which was the cause of her migraines, her vagaries, even the eye trouble, all the weakness that Mme Roché despised?

This is the story given in Chapter XIII of *Two English Girls and the Continent*. It is told without authorial intervention, except for one interesting moment. When Muriel/Margaret describes pleasuring herself at the age of seventeen, as she lies under the cobalt sky, poppies swaying around her, he has one of his infrequent footnotes: 'See page 161.' The reference is to Chapter XI ('The Separation') which evokes Claude's holiday in Austria after his banishment from Muriel, the period described in Pierre's Collins Golden Notebook. He is in the Alps in the summer of 1902, deer-hunting with Austrian friends, sleeping out. One morning he wakes before dawn. The sun rises astonishingly and Claude ejaculates, or 'gives himself'; to the mountainside. It is what Freud would call an oceanic experience. This is the period in the lives of Claude/Pierre and Muriel/Margaret in which they were keeping journals about what it was like to be parted. In this section of his novel Roché uses two columns to the page, an ingenious 'split-screen' technique, to show what both were thinking. On page 161 we have Muriel on the left and Claude on the right.

In the middle of tennis, which Claude loves, after two sets, I had trouble seeing and had to go in and lie on my bed. I would love to be active, gay, indefatigable! Should I start taking siestas again?	Obedient to I know not what command, I put down my rifle and *came* into all this beauty, of which you were a part, Muriel. I think that you do not know this word.

The right-hand column is amplified by a footnote: 'Claude only knew two years later, from the "Confession" of Muriel, that one day a similar type of communion overwhelmed her, stretched out on her back, deep in the corn, face up to the blue of the sky.'

Muriel/Margaret was never able simply to accept her 'communions' as joys. However, in reality, once Margaret had sent 'The Confession' to Pierre, her journal was cheerful; the action of confessing appears to have been more affirmative than the content of 'The Confession'. She wrote about dread and shame, but it seems that she felt excited, validated. She had in a sense *joined* Pierre: she, too, had confessed; she, too, had a sexuality. The act of confession equalised them. There was some triumph in it, as seen in Stacey Tendeter's performance as Muriel/Margaret in Truffaut's film.

Soon after the confession Margaret wrote in her diary, 'I have just come back from choir practice – a *delight*. I begin to really honestly enjoy life again.' She was 'glad for once to be without Pierre', enjoying the 'condition of Absence'. She wrote

appreciatively about Violet, her beauty, that of her *face*, she hastened to add. She had in the past praised 'dear old Violet' occasionally for being a good sister; now she was admiring her 'person'. But this buoyancy did not last. On what could she *use* its energy? In her journal she began to berate her life as a household drudge, and misery crept back.

> My God, oh my God, what is to be done? If only I could get away from Mother – and do hard regular work. Here it is *so* hard to get out of this black depression, this *languor*, this misery which is taking over my whole being.

In the journal Margaret occasionally wrote in French, and she now uses the word *dépression* for the first time. It was new to English in its modern sense (i.e., a psychological syndrome rather than a metaphor for low spirits). The *Oxford English Dictionary* defines one meaning of 'depression' by giving a quotation from the *Psychological Review* of 1905: 'Symptoms of depression, the motor retardation, the difficulty of apprehension, become aggravated in various forms of melancholia.' Despite the vitality of her confession to Pierre (had she not matched his?), depression was the pit into which Margaret now sank.

Chapter Three

the sisters

Margaret struggled with illness and depression in England
during 1903. Pierre was now settled in Paris, writing and
translating and making new woman friends. Violet was established at art school in Paris, with a bare attic studio of her own,
whose emptiness appealed to the aesthetically ascetic Pierre. He
saw her occasionally and a year or so passed before they again
made an impact upon each other. Pierre liked to call her
'Mauve', perhaps because English middle-class people associated the colour mauve with 'being artistic'. She knew about
Germaine, now established as Pierre's regular, tolerant mistress.
He had seriously explained to Violet that he believed it was
disgusting to wish exclusively to control a woman. She was no
longer *aide de camp* for Margaret. Violet had intrigued Pierre
since 1899 when she first raised her lorgnette to him at Arago.

One afternoon in February 1904 Pierre went to see some
sketches at Violet's studio. Just home, she was flushed by
the stairs, her heart beating fast, as was Pierre's. He remembered
the agile way she climbed at Conway Castle and the jerk of her
shoulder against the recoil of a rifle at a shooting-range
in Switzerland. He placed a hand tentatively against the
painting-smock she was wearing under her coat. One of her
hands rose as if to remove it, but she enclosed his palm and led it
to her right breast. There was a knock at the door. Violet knew
that a maid from Mme Roché was expected. The couple were
silent until the caller had gone, then Violet spoke, using *tu* to

Pierre for the first time. She said she had to leave Paris soon, but they could stay together in Switzerland in the summer. They agreed to a holiday in a cabin by Lake Lucerne later in the year. With this pact they parted.

Pierre started travelling again. Violet first went to Kingsnorth, then to stay with friends in Chelsea, and, after pleadings from her mother, back to Kingsnorth. Where and when could she paint there? Margaret was so ill that she was needed. Violet's relationship with Pierre had entered a period of suspension, rather like Margaret's after the enforced separation, but at least she could write to him. In Hungary and Italy Pierre received a tumult of letters, sometimes about the Kent countryside (like Samuel Palmer paintings in prose), sometimes about Pierre's 'free and healthy love' ('amour libre, amour sain') which she wanted to share. She wrote him a prose poem with an erotic line of trailing dashes in it.

Bees are coming with sacs of pollen to drop into the heart of the flowers. And I, what is it I can see in front of me at the end of this long green, someone who is near and coming closer? Ah! It is he who loves me and the one I love. Flowers, bees, trees vanish, I throw back my head. Sun! Love! Am I supposed to be ashamed? No, I am *not*. No! No! Love that is free and sound cannot live like a prisoner, it bathes me in a gold, but a hot shower, burning hot with such a dazzling light that I know I am fainting. I cannot see. I cannot see him any more. All I can see is the grass. I am just light and heat.

— —

My Lover, where is he? He has vanished, but no, am I dreaming? Reality is a dream, and dreams are more real than life.

The last sentence echoes what Margaret wrote at the beginning of her Paris journal: 'Do not forget that much of this belongs to the life of the imagination.'

Violet told Pierre she was reading Flaubert's *Salammbô*. She went over the history of her friendship with Pierre, remembering herself as the younger sister who was admired for her singing voice, but not Pierre's preferred girl, though she did think, correctly, that he wanted to kiss her at Conway. She had had short-lived jealousies of Margaret, and was intrigued, but not shocked, when she learned the truth about Pierre and Pilar, the truth Margaret said would have outraged their brother, Stephen. She wrote to Pierre that she felt she was 'morally timid, but physically brave, good for nothing but to be a soldier', a vocation which interested her. She did read Tolstoy on non-violence, but was no longer 'hostile, as before, to everything to do with war'. She was curious about Germaine, admiring how she and Pierre seemed to manage to be a couple. She wrote that because she needed him, she wanted to be close to Germaine as well. Could she join them in a friendship to form a new and different trio? Because love was an art-form for Pierre.

It was at this point that Violet was allowed to use independently her father's money which had hitherto been held in trust for her. Life at Kingsnorth became increasingly irksome, especially the necessity of being secret about Pierre. She asked him to use a typewriter for his letters to her and that their envelopes be addressed to Margaret who could not sort the mail because her sight was too bad. One day a cousin took Violet out in his motor car which broke down two hours from home. He picked over the engine and got it going, but Violet had the sensation of impending disaster, such as a runaway crash down a hill-side, or petrol burns. She realised with chagrin that she had thought only about her painting and Pierre, not for a moment of her family. She wrote to him that if he lost interest in her, she would neither kill herself nor 'retire into the arms of my family'. She knew how Pierre organised his loves, but she possessed the stoic excitement of a younger child who knows it is not the end of the world to be second, and anyway sees a chance of defeating the eldest. Violet was annoyed with herself for staying so long in Kent with the endless 'bazaars' and hearing 'Oh Violet, are you painting *again*?' or 'Now we have a puppy for you to train!' She had to read to Margaret. 'Violet is my eyes.' Pierre's letters were a tonic, like cold baths or French coffee. 'I love them, *mon garçon*', she wrote, like the working girl in D. H. Lawrence's *Sons and Lovers* who calls Paul Morel 'my boy'.

At long last came the summer of 1904 and the reunion with Pierre. Violet became his lover in the middle of June. She arrived in Switzerland by train and they travelled to the isolated lake-side cabin where they were to stay for ten days. Our knowledge of this episode depends entirely upon Roché's account in *Two English Girls and the Continent*. Violet was now unusually talkative. She had worked out what she thought – principally that she would under no circumstances go down the path taken by or forced upon Margaret who was struggling with illness at home. Violet had been reading Malthus, wanted to borrow Rémy de Gourmont from Pierre and had decided she would rather make statues than babies, and that she would become a *useful* artist, like G. F. Watts. She said she was frightened about these ideas, suspecting she would be even more frightened once she started to put them into practice. They slept separately, until Violet said she would like to be in bed with Pierre. They had been talking about friends and whether the word *copain* was 'vulgar'. Pierre explained that it was not, but was a student word, one warmer and more cute ('drôle') than *camarade*. 'Are we *copains*?' she asked. He said that they were, except that friends in this sense did not feel their hearts pounding when they were together, a fire which could change them. 'So be it,' said Violet. 'Straight away.'

After they made love Violet said that this was a game 'which cancelled out all others', but it had not been 'us'. It was as if Pierre had been playing for himself. She asked if it would always be like that. They would wait and see, said Pierre. He suggested they stay at Lake Lucerne for a few more days. Violet said they should do what they had meant to and part. 'We are free, and this is so beautiful.'

(This lake-side idyll is one of the most endearing episodes in Truffaut's film of *Two English Girls and the Continent*. At the beginning a long travelling shot follows Anne/Violet carrying a stick like a little soldier and Claude/Pierre pottering by the lake. There is perhaps too much humour solicited by Claude's discomfiture at the sight of Anne's clumsy flannel night-gown, but the love-making is swiftly and affectionately portrayed. 'A light barrier breaks.' The couple separate sportingly, rowing two dinghies away to opposite sides of the screen, a vignette epitomising this summertime beauty of freedom.)

In the autumn Violet was back home in Kingsnorth. Pierre wrote teasing her, but earnestly, that she was becoming a slave to Court family values. She was managing to paint, she replied, but there is 'more truth in you, Pierre, than in painting.' She would soon be back in Paris: 'Do not come to see me unless you want to.' Soon after Christmas he went to his apartment on Rue d'Alésia with a girl-friend and found letters from Violet franked in Paris. She wrote that she was thrilled to be back, because in Kingsnorth she had to paint herself in a mirror, but now she could use live models again. Pierre went straight round to her attic. The door was open and Violet was in profile when he entered, which he thought emphasised the sadness he associated with her, which 'penetrated his heart'. 'Her eyes don't look, but wait,' he thought. Pierre showed her a photograph of Viève. 'She is pretty,' Violet inevitably said. Their love affair resumed.

Now, in January 1905, the attraction between Pierre and Violet became consuming for both of them. Violet's side of the affair is shown in a letter of 27 March, written for once in English. When Roché re-read it, years later, he inscribed one of his red-inked notes on it: *Vio. en feu – sweet.* Violet wrote:

Don't read this until you are willing to be disturbed and can come and see me soon.

Mon Pierre – I don't want you to come before it is quite convenient – but oh! I do want you terribly badly – and one little visit won't do me any good – it would only make your absence harder to bear. The longing I have for you – oh, I can't stand it much longer.

When you have finished with the reviews, which I curse against my will for preventing you from coming to see me, then please, if you can, do try to come often to see me for a little while. I was wretched nearly the whole time in England

and thought things would be better here – but it is just the same. Oh, I have brought my unhappiness with me – and I *can't* throw it off. Do help me! And don't scold me too much.

I go about the streets – I try to work – I hardly sleep – I try to find comfort in the acquaintances within my reach, but they bring me none – they all say how well I look (this is because I am red in the face) and they don't see the misery underneath.

I know I am the only one that can help myself – unless it is you – tell me, where do you find comfort and strength when you feel as bad as I do now? Is your trouble never greater than yourself? Is there always a bit of you left over to put things right?

The worst of it is, as I can't see a reason, I can't see a remedy except, *you*, yes, *you*, *you* – and if I can't have you – and if nothing else brings me to myself again, I feel as if I should go mad. Oh, why can't I have you now and keep you as long as I wish!

Don't come before you are ready, but the minute you have finished your necessary work, do come home as quickly as you can, even if it is twelve at night.

I should like to go to Norway alone with you and watch the midnight sun or in the mountains with no soul but you. It would be a foolish thing to do, quite contrary to reasoning, but it is wise to do unwise things sometimes. Do you know I believe there is only one place where I should not be thus haunted by the poverty in me – the vacant blackness inhabited only by these longings – and that place is *wherever* you and I happened to be together.

When one feels very, very worthless – does it mean that one's idea of value has been raised? I feel so incapable that my reason asks what is the good of my living.

Our love has brought me this. Yes – I see it! That is it! Formerly I thought I was something because I was blind – now that I am able to distinguish what was before invisible to me, I see that I am nothing at all. Nature is strange that she prevents us from throwing ourselves into the sea.

So! I expect you on Monday at 2.30. Could you arrange

things so that it were possible for you to remain away from home the whole night if we wished it? If so and you would like to dine in my studio, let me know. I am not free tomorrow Sunday afternoon from two to four. Unless you tell me in the morning that you could come – and then I could put off the engagement easily.

   Good-bye

    Your Mauve

      – to do what you like with, and sometimes against my will, it seems to me. This paper is your skin – and the ink my blood – pressing hard so that the marks can never be rubbed out. Oh dear, I am certainly half off my head. Do you feel it? Does it hurt? Things change in such a funny way, the air that presses against my lips is hot, like fire.

Pierre was absorbed by Violet in these weeks, a changed woman who 'knows how to use herself, to tighten her arms, twist her body. She knows how to string me out ("m' étendre"), completely, powerfully, sending me into waves of vertigo.' Her former passivity ('terrible inertie') had disappeared. She was now in Pierre's vocabulary 'Woman-Woman'. However, Violet went back to Kingsnorth for Easter 1905, and while they resumed when she returned, Pierre noted in his journal a touch of 'habitude'.

One evening towards the end of April they made love for three hours, almost ritually ('comme une messe'). He especially watched the movements of her arms. They then went out to a party given by a female Russian artist, Toulka. Violet was now neither boyish nor school-girlish, with her hair cut more elegantly, and shining eyes. She was closely observed by a well-known Russian figure in their circle, Maksimilian Voloshinov, nicknamed 'Mouff', who in Roché's novel and Truffaut's film is called 'Diurka'. In the film he is a sensuous, curly-haired character, played by a good-looking actor, Philippe Léotard. In reality Max was powerfully handsome, with long hair, heavy beard and an eccentric-professor manner. He looked bulky in photographs and 'cube-shaped', according to Pierre who, as a boxer, noticed Max had three times his own biceps. Though only thirty years old, he was already a well-known Symbolist poet, and also painter, critic, traveller (mirroring Pierre in this). Among Toulka's candles, rugs, cigarette smoke and sofas, he had, thought Pierre, the appearance of a Herculean slave of whom Violet could be the owner. Pierre knew young women liked Max and loved to listen to him talk about Anthroposophy. Through the party gloom Pierre watched Violet across the room on a divan with Max seated on the floor by her. He put his huge head on her lap. Pierre tried saying to himself, 'Why not?' Violet later stroked Max's mane; then the three of them were together on a sofa, Violet's gown loosened across her breasts. Absinthe went round; the groups changed and merged. Max, Violet and Toulka were enlaced together. Pierre's hand was led to a woman's corsage, but then diverted by another hand. He saw Violet who kissed him, asking if he was happy. 'I think so. And you?' 'Yes.' Pierre's hand was taken anew, down to touch the sex of a girl closely enough for him to be able to tell she was a virgin. He said in his journal he was less happy than he had intimated to Violet. He was erotically a daylight person, disdaining people who took each other with absinthe. He wondered if Violet liked this sort of touching, being almost sure that she did not. When it started to get light, Pierre made his move, leaving Violet, Toulka and Max together under a tapestry rug. He gulped the morning air and noticed Max's famous painted bicycle. He carefully deflated its tyres.

When Pierre went to Violet's attic the next day there was no answer, nor the day after. He decided correctly she was there with Max, or at Max's studio. (Truffaut was particularly touched by this incident, and aesthetically sensitive to the visual intrigue in which a character ascends stairs and has to retreat when a door is meaningfully not answered. It happens in *Anne and Muriel*, in *Stolen Kisses* and there is a version of it in *Shoot the Piano Player*.)

On 4 May Violet was home and answered his knock. Pierre put his hands on her shoulders as usual, but she shook her head: 'Not to-day.' He knew what had happened, but was hungry for details. 'Max?' Violet hid her head on his shoulder; Pierre gently stroked her neck. She had not left the party with him, but Max had come to her attic after Toulka's 'little orgy' and they spent four days together, surely as Pierre the love-philosopher would have done? 'It was a shock,' said Pierre. 'I had you first, when you were a virgin. But I approve. It is completely all right.' Max had been interested for some time, she said, planning to approach her when she returned to Paris after Easter. He said he wanted to live with her. He did not mind if she became pregnant, said Violet. Pierre started to leave, but Violet shouted after him to come back. They made 'frénétique' love. Afterwards they had English tea in their customary way: they agreed she would now go with Max. Pierre was disturbed by what was happening, though he said Max was a decent ('propre') man. He asked Violet if Max was 'précis', a special word of his meaning sexually 'exact' in making love. 'Not in the same way.' She said she had suffered about Viève. Pierre's journal reads.

Violet: Are you going to suffer now?
Me: It gives me more joy than pain.
    She repeated the words.

So, thought Pierre, she had left him behind; so much the better. He was a little 'proud of his work' with her, not altogether perhaps a vain or male perception: a lover is able to imagine him or herself beaming with pleasure to see a former lover with a successor, feeling that he or she has prepared the way.

Violet told Pierre she would go to Turkey with Max and this she did. But the relationship did not last long. In September 1905 she wrote from Russia that Mouff was now only a friend and he married later in that year. Pierre had, of course, his girl-friends in Paris and the reliable succour of Viève. When Violet returned in November, shaken by her Russian experience, she continued to be needy for sex with him. Once when they were smoking in bed, she said that losing her virginity had been a gift to her. Now Pierre found himself thinking of another woman (usually Germaine) scarcely had they finished making love. Sleep became difficult for him with Violet, or sleep after sex which he called 'love-schlep', an integral part of erotic experience for Roché. Sometimes Violet sent him a *pneumatique* telegram commanding him to come without delay. Pierre noted that now it was Violet who grieved ('groaned', wrote Pierre in English) as he had done when she told him she wanted Max. She had other lovers, most regularly Todia, a young Russian artist who lived across the landing from her attic. She told Pierre that Todia was married, but his wife wanted a free union.

It was now over two years since the climax of the separation between Margaret and Pierre, that is, Margaret's confession of 'Solitary Vice'. 'The Confession', with its declaration that she was not 'une fille intacte', had been important because Margaret stood up for herself, albeit by means of self-accusation. She had put on record what she believed herself to be and had thus *outdone* the confessions of Pierre (first about Pilar, then the whole of the Collins Golden Notebook). But the exhilaration of confession did not last. At Kingsnorth she became progressively weaker and her sight deteriorated again, until she was completely blind in both eyes. It was difficult to move about the house; she did not even want to be read to, and she adopted a strict vegetarian diet. However, early in 1905, when Violet and Pierre were deepest into their passion in Paris, she began to improve and gained strength as she moderated the diet. A book which revitalised her was a popular work of American religiosity (in print even today), *In Tune with the Infinite, or, Fullness of Peace and Power and Plenty* by Ralph Waldo Trine who was gushingly positive in a vein of vague spiritualism about the 'God-thoughts' which inspire 'God-power'. (Later the younger sisters of the novelist Ivy Compton-Burnett, Topsy and Primrose, also depressives, were devotees of Trine. His book was found in the room in which they committed suicide.) In the autumn of 1905 Margaret wrote a free verse poem in stumbling pencilled handwriting very different from her bold ink-penning of the past:

No wave sighed out, now broke the grey with foam,
Sand dunes sloped gently up from the shore
Crowned with sea-grasses, wizened, harsh and thin,
Sea poppies crouched, low on the sterile soil,
Mourning the golden flowers they yearned to bear.
That was long years ago, our dance of death,
Long years ago. But still I cannot see
Flat sands, stilled waves, under a low grey sky,
But when I see I turn away to fear
Before the memory, shuddering that stirs
The memory of our dance of death and love,
That dance of anguish, hopelessness and love.

After Christmas she was more cheerful, and could see a little with both eyes and in January 1906 she once again experimented with a journal, expressing herself with neither the idealism nor the defiance of her previous ones. She started by writing that she was dubious of a human being doing self-analysis. 'While one admires it when applied to the study of plants or beasts or social laws, one feels one should condemn it when applied to one's inner life', but 'anyway, I *shall* write'. She resolved to try to be true to her scientific training at school, the experience later 'greatly fostered and trained by the Charity Organisation Society' in London. She was now well enough to travel to meet Violet at Kelèse in Switzerland: and to address the problem of Pierre again. Four years had passed since Pierre's experiment with life in London. Violet and Margaret had now a new and less timid Pierre to contend with.

In the spring of 1906 Pierre received a letter from Violet announcing that she had been in Kingsnorth and was returning to Paris with Margaret whose health had much improved. Pierre still thought of Margaret as his 'grand amour passé', the red-headed one, the 'Rousse', whose image he sought in other women. When he read the letter he remembered how he sometimes used to feel his chest would burst when he was with her. On 4 May the sisters arrived in Paris without forewarning Pierre. He received a note informing him that Margaret had arrived and was ready to meet him. He went to Violet's attic expecting to find the sisters, but there was no Violet and he was taken aback to discover that it was the last day, indeed the last hour, of Margaret's stay in Paris. She said to him simply after three years of illness, 'It's me.' She told him that she had been blind for two years, but that she had been able to see for a few weeks. She was wearing the tinted spectacles with which he was familiar. They talked clumsily for about ten minutes. Pierre started to make his farewell. Then Margaret crossed the room and kissed him. He was astounded, but told his journal that he did not feel attraction exactly, but some desire moved, the 'old wound' hurting. 'Is she beautiful?' he asked. 'No.' But 'the pride of her simple demeanour, the vigour of her body and the shape of her head, her high eye-brows which she raises so animatedly, and those eyes. Her low voice is unforgettable, and can have such gaiety.' In *Two English Girls and the Continent* this meeting is described in a chapter called 'Le Long Baiser', alluding to Rodin's *The Kiss*. According to Margaret's journal, they embraced for nearly an hour 'travelling together in a kiss'. She thought Pierre was sensitive to the consent in her lips, but not aware of 'mon amour constant'. He wrote that evening in his journal that he said to her 'I loved you so much, but not I love you'. Then Violet returned because she had arranged, astutely it seems, that Margaret should soon leave for Gare du Nord. She was to collect her sister and help her down the stairs with her bag. On the journey to the coast Margaret said she felt good for nothing. 'He is racing in my heart,' she wrote later: 'Il galope en moi.'

Margaret's arrival in Paris and the kiss was momentous for her. For Pierre it was fascinating, but also an interruption to the delightful life he had established in the democratic, sociable, crowded art world in which one social unit was the girl with a man on each arm. George du Maurier showed it in *Trilby* and his friend Felix Moscheles neatly illustrated it in his book about the life of artists in Paris and Brussels with a little sketch of the standard bohemian trio of an earlier generation which none the less was emblematic of Pierre's world.

Pierre frequented Closerie des Lilas, the literary café domi-
nated by André Salmon, editor of *Vers et Prose*, which published
some of his writing. He kept up his boxing. In Paris he 'knew
everyone'. Henri Pierre Roché was the one who in 1905 had
taken Picasso across the city to introduce him to the novelist
Gertrude Stein and her brother Leo, whom he especially liked
and whose conversations he once planned to make into a book.
Pierre travelled and was swiftly able to assume local coloration.
Picasso commented on his chameleon nature: Roché, he said,
was not a person, but a translation.

One incident in his relationship with Gertrude Stein is vividly
revealing about the new Pierre. Stein coined for him the name
'Vrais', based on *vrai*, meaning the candid, fastidious one. 'A
very earnest, very noble, devoted, very faithful and enthusiastic
man.' She added that 'one need never see him again, but one
knows that somewhere Roché is faithful.' Roché admired Stein's
novel *Three Lives*, about ordinary American people: two im-
migrant German servant women and Melanctha, a black woman
in love with a black doctor. She emulated in her prose Cézanne's
'dispassionate' portraiture, each thing in a composition as important as each other thing, a form of visual meditation by
means of repetition. (She wrote at a desk which faced one of the
finest paintings she and Leo had acquired, Cézanne's *Portrait of
Madame Cézanne*.) Roché loved Cézanne, but had his reserva-
tions about Stein's 'prose-painting'. He wrote to her as follows:

The other day you told me about this girl at the Vendôme Tea Room. It was a good story. I had a good laugh. Then, suddenly, you say it again shorter, but the same. You spoil my laugh. I ask myself: 'Why does she say it again?' I get angry with you to spoil it for me by those damned repetitions. Many repetitions have great purpose and efficiency, but they have a sea of sisters, which, I think, have perceivable meaning for nobody but you.

I start reading your style only when I am very strong and want in a way to suffer. After a few minutes I am giddy, then sea-sick, though there are islands to be seen. It is no river, no sea: it is a winter flood in the country. Rhythm? Ah, yes. But that sort of rhythm is intoxicating you – it is something like masturbation.

Of course it is very enjoyable to let oneself go and write heaps, but – why don't you finish, correct, re-write ten times the same chaotic material till it has its very shape worthy of its fullness? A condensation of 60% to 90% would often do.

Do you know anyone (human, not literary) who, without knowing you, or the models of your portraits, or both, has understood something in them?

Melanctha in *Three Women* is great in my memory. I was quite at home with her, though I had already some toil. I thought your style would concentrate: it has enormously expanded.

The last things stand on the strength of your personality, far from my eyes, they fall to pieces.

Your own right faith in yourself shakes other people's doubts about your ways of expression – they probably do not tell them much in front of you?

Are you not after all very lazy?

Roché signed off 'with frankness, humility and perhaps huge stupidity', a stylised diffidence which did not work with Stein who was not without self-importance. (Picasso did a painting for her called *Hommage à Gertrude Stein* which pictures her blowing her own minuscule trumpet.) Communication between Roché and Stein thereafter ceased for eight years, not surprisingly because his letter shows an aesthetic philosophy at variance with Stein's in its valuation of sincerity, a directness of treatment in which the artist seems to stand aside.

Absence of ego was a mark of the new Pierre as a writer and in his conscientiously pursued love-affairs in which he seemed to cancel his prior self, approaching women not as if there were no tomorrow, but as if there were no yesterday, no script in which they were participating. One of the commentators on Roché's life, Manfred Flügge, in his study of the background to *Jules and Jim*, remarks on the apparent oddity of his life as a lover. He says Roché was an 'unlikely Casanova', one who fixated upon specificities, an ear, a wrist, a movement of the lip which arrested him for the moment, obliterating previous occasions and people, including the ones from whom and in whom he had just come. (One wonders what is a likely Casanova.) Flügge's theory is that journal-writing and serial loving have affinities: every day a new start. Picasso once said to Roché that at the start of a painting 'I throw myself naked into the water: I swim, I find.' Roché remembered this at the end of his life when he saw Henri-Georges Clouzot's film *The Picasso Mystery* in 1956, which he thought perfectly demonstrated this insight into the painting process.

In Paris a new Pierre was developing, one facet of whom was now the beginnings of a life of curious psychological service or surrender to the moment which made him amusing, loyal and collaborative. There were some steady factors, notably in his regular Thursday afternoons, evenings and nights with Viève, but none more stabilising than a friendship which began in 1906 with the man who was to be portrayed much later as Jules in *Jules and Jim*. Pierre found in Franz Hessel a successor to Jo Jouanin, someone peaceable, ingenious, scholarly and who, like himself, was a 'man who loved women', though he often struck the wrong note with them.

Franz Hessel was German, about Pierre's own age (born in 1880 to a Polish Jewish family made wealthy from the grain trade). His parents settled in the German port of Stettin and later in Berlin where by 1900 they had converted to Lutheranism. Franz was, like Pierre, a convert to Protestantism, and one of four children. The eldest and youngest boys were models of assimilated Jews, influential in banking and education and later a natural target for the

German right wing. The daughter, Annie, was a favourite of Franz and died young. Franz became the poet of the family, committed to language and letters, especially to Greek antiquities, though a Modernist. Before he met Pierre he had lived for three years in Schwabing, the Montparnasse of Munich, with Stefan George and the Symbolists. He returned to Berlin where he started a literary review, *Vers und Prosa*, thence departing for Paris to the circle of Apollinaire in which he met Pierre.

Franz and Pierre enjoyed going around with the young painter Marie Laurencin whom they met soon after the arrival of Franz in Paris. Franz sometimes said he loved her, then absent-mindedly forgot he had said so (or even that he did). Marie Laurencin was in her early twenties and painted with ink lines and washes in the mundanely other-world manner of Chagall; not a Gertrude Stein style at all. As a person she was 'direct, frank, and talked tough' with a lower lip Pierre thought irresistible: 'a wide mouth, turning up at the corners, then suddenly, right in the middle, the lower lip becomes very full.' She would go to the Alésia apartment and ask questions about the women who had been there including whether they were virgins like herself. She listened carefully to Pierre's descriptions and explanations of love-making. She told him how the girls at her *lycée* talked sometimes about masturbating which Marie found distasteful. Pierre's journal shows the three of them together, with Marie as 'Flap' and Franz as 'Glob'. This is an entry for 26 November 1906.

Franz's room. He, Flap, and I. Flap begins to rummage through Glob's closet, shows off his neck-ties, and makes us laugh. Tea. Flap dances, shows her lovely legs, lets down her hair, throws herself across Glob's big bed. On each side of her, at a distance, Glob and I stretch out and each takes one of her hands.

Glob and Flap sing softly to each other. With her eyes fixed on Glob, Flap moves closer to me, and the movements of her hand ask for caresses. I caress. First her arm and her thigh. Darkness is falling. They continue to sing. My finger reaches her sex, closed then suddenly half-open, and Flap, still singing, trembles a little. My caress is light.

I get up to leave. Finally she looks at me. Her expression frightens me.

I leave them together for the evening.

In the end it was Pierre with whom Marie first had sex. When she kissed, he noticed how her face became redder. He wrote in his journal how much she resembled himself at the age of sixteen, before he started meeting girls with Jo by means of their advertisements. She, too, was 'neurasthénique', with a tragic quality in her face. 'The female is being born and is trembling inside her.' Later Marie became the lover of Apollinaire, who was, wrote Pierre, more 'manly' than himself or Franz. In 1914 she married the German painter Otto von Watjen, migrating for the duration of the war to Spain.

We are able to eavesdrop on an afternoon with 'Flap' and 'Glob' courtesy of Roché's journal, his definitive journal, that is, not his early diary in which he described his adventures with the girls for whom he advertised, and his experiment in jealousy with Jo Jouanin. This definitive journal was begun in 1904, in notebooks known as the *Carnets*, which proliferated down the years, and of which a typed copy was made after Roché's death by François Truffaut. This journal is a rich source of information about Roché's life, but its creation was also an event or sequence of events in that life: the journal was *of* his life, like a very long-term lover, like Viève. It was kept in slender grey pocket-books, preferably of English manufacture. Roché made title and contents pages for them, and carefully marked on the latter when he re-read his old texts. The following is an extract from the Carnet XXXII, from 28 November to 27 December 1906, as is stated on a title page. It shows the contents page for *7 December and 12 December (Mauve)* – 'Mauve' was of course Violet. It shows what life was like in the weeks during which Roché spent his afternoons with Marie and Franz. On each title page there would be a careful inscription that, if found, the diary should be returned to 99 Rue d'Arago, where a reward would be given. (The address of the family apartment was given to keep the notebooks safe from the eyes of lovers. Mme Roché disdained to be inquisitive.)

CARNET XXXII

<u>RELU A BELLEVUE</u> – <u>10 AVRIL 1934</u> – <u>ET AU CAP FERRET 23 MAI '34</u>

Visite à SBO – Bordel. **MAUVE**. FLAP chez FREDE.
Tout cela sert à grandir VIEVE – GLOB et FLAP et GYA.

<u>MAUVE</u>: 7/12 – 12/12 –

Jaloux d'Opia un soir. – GLOB et FLAP et moi. –
OPIA et TIS (P.F.). – La nuit CETTE, GLOB, OPIA en moi, finir
chastement en AL ESIA. – Départ imminent de GLOB.
Jolies nervosités de FLAP entre lui et moi. – VIEVE
centre charmant. – Propos pour l'amour entre FLAP et moi. –
Tout un après-midi chez OPIA. Grande caresse et demi fiasco
amical. – REIA en ALESIA: déception, rhume, odeur. – Prise
totale de FLAP: Don-Juan et Ophélie. – Bal masqué à la
Palette. Re-MAUVE, en passant . . .
Déjeuner à MONTMARTRE avec VIEVE, après mort de son Juge.
Une heure avec SBO: je la situe mieux. – Une belle rencontre
imprévue a vec MAGA. – Une visite de SBO.

- - - - - - - - - - - - - - - - - - - -

L'ensemble du récit est naturel, franc et coulant.
Pour moi, il reproduit bien ma vie d'alors.

There are two interesting aspects to this contents page: first, at the beginning Roché says that sex with the other people serves to elevate ('grandir') his sense of the best friend of all, Viève, and second, at the end he expresses satisfaction in this particular *Carnet*, written in a style 'natural, frank, and flowing'. This was exactly what his life then was like, he added later.

This life was to be breached once again by the person with whom he thought he had settled accounts. Margaret Court did not forget the kiss and came to visit him again.

Having crossed the room and kissed Pierre, a perspective opened out for Margaret, made fresher by the fact that life in the coming months was easier in Kingsnorth. There was a new servant so she had more time. She promised herself this would not be the last meeting with Pierre. In January 1907 she sent him a book and at the beginning of March wrote to him showing that she still loved him. He wrote in his journal that he could not forget 'Nuk' either. Violet had talked to him about her sister's illnesses, saying that she thought that she suffered from lack of love. Pierre wrote to Margaret saying he wanted to see her, and Violet wrote, too, encouraging her to come to Paris. She did so in late March 1907.

Margaret stayed in Violet's attic, meeting the artists of the Café Russe group. She became quite friendly with Todia, Violet's occasional lover. She went again to see Rodin's *The Kiss* and wondered about it, herself and Pierre. Could they kiss like that? But there was no sign of Pierre for a fortnight. He was ill, said Violet. Then came extraordinary news. Violet brought a note from Pierre which said: 'We have everything in the world to talk about. Come for a week in Brittany with me as soon as I am better.' Hardly believing what she was doing, Margaret wrote and agreed. Pierre replied, asking her to see him at Alésia, which she had never visited before, on Thursday 22 March. Violet proposed on the Wednesday that they should walk there – she intended, anyway, she said, to deliver Pierre some English medicine – so Margaret would be sure to know the way. The girls duly arrived at the apartment block on Rue d'Alésia. Violet rather hastily ushered Margaret on to a returning bus and went up to the apartment. In her imagination Margaret saw Violet ascending the stairs. Back at home, she waited.

At this point Margaret can relate what happened. Not much later she wrote up the day's events as a story. We have heard Margaret's voice as a writer before, in extracts from her Paris journal and later in extracts from her story of Pierre's final departure from Kingsnorth at the beginning of the separation; we have read some of her description of London life, notably of the 'elephant man'. Margaret's story about her visit to Paris in 1907 is written with an emotional freedom which is very different from Roché's terseness. It may be hard for the reader to make the transition from a Roché-orientated narrative to that of the excited, bewildered young woman in whom thoughts of Pierre still 'galloped'. She wrote her story in English. Violet appears as 'Katherine' (compare 'Catherine' in *Wuthering Heights* and *Jules and Jim*). Margaret has her own name, or 'Maggie' or 'Meg'. Violet's Todia appears under his real name, as does another friend, Nina, and a well-known Russian artist, Krouglikoff, a woman whom Margaret had met with the Café Russe people. In the story the place in which Pierre proposes they spend a week together is transformed from Brittany to Holland. (I have made a few small amendments or deletions when Margaret's writing is illegible, or her meaning gets momentarily lost in the rush to say what happened.)

How long Katherine stays! Well Maggie knows that time flies with Pierre and she smiles wistfully and whispers 'Darling' just above her breath. She has taken his taboret and perches on it in the wide open window, her elbows on her knees, her chin in her hands. How quiet the court is. It seems to her that there was no sound, that the rare passers-by crossed the street arch to the inner court without a footfall: as silently as the white and grey cats, they crossed the court and disappeared. In the window of the third storey, away there in the far corner, is a large crimson lampshade. How softly it glows in the warm dusk! How kind of its little dark-eyed mistress to light it within sight. Now the man who stood in the window opposite has gone and closed his windows and Maggie seems the only watcher.

She jumps from the stool, shuddering. *Madame Roché is there again and a revolver is held near her head.* She does not want to die! [Not] now that she has given herself in thought, in promise as Pierre's wife, with that wonderful week in Holland [in prospect] for which all the past seems but the preparation. Ah, no: she cannot die. Who is in the court? Pierre and Katherine? Quick as thought she is over to the rail, gripping it tight, hanging there. She calls, but, ceasing to pace the dark room, she forces her thoughts back to reality and perches herself again in the window. Now there are footfalls and every moment she strains her eyes looking up for the tall thin form and the shorter one beside it, the two she waits for and longs to see, surely soon.

Ah! what a perfect corner this is; how quiet, how sincere, how in tune with all within her. All the world seems wonderful to the little woman as she leans there, secure at last in happiness after the bitter suffering, after the weary waiting, after the hopes through darkness, the trust through silence. All that is behind, all that is well past, and only makes the present seem more wonderful, more perfect. To be loved by Pierre, to love passionately at last and to dare to love completely. She is then a true woman, a complete creature of God. She steps from the stool on to her knees. Thank God for Pierre – oh! I thank Thee, I thank Thee for Pierre and Katherine – God bless Pierre and Katherine.

There is a knock at the door. Nina has come to say good-bye. She has only just seen her way to shake hands by the light coming in from the other windows, dimly. She speaks warmly, even affectionately and gives a bouquet wrapped in white paper. Maggie excited, off her balance, hurries down the stairs leaving the door wide open. They stand shaking hands on the pavement in the full moonlight, under the little court trees that are already in bud. 'Ah! *voilà* Katherine!' Nina exclaims and Maggie looks up from the darkness beyond the lamp light.

Katherine comes. She walks constrainedly, but her head is not bent. She smiles and as she reaches them she puts her hand on Maggie's shoulder. Never has Maggie felt that touch before: she did not understand it; she felt and appreciated the affection; its compassion she could not know! The hand lingers a long moment on her shoulder while Katherine smiles and speaks not to Maggie, but to Nina, and Maggie, remembering the open door, rushes gaily upstairs. There, she lights the lamps and puts on the prepared supper-table her gorgeous bunch of single yellow daffodils.

They had finished their supper and sat still at the table. Katherine sat with her elbows on the table, her forehead leaning on both hands. There had been something unusual in the air, but there was nothing but small talk over the surface of Katherine's visit to Pierre: 'Had she seen the spirit stove?' 'Was his throat better?' and so on. Now there was a long silence.

Maggie pushed her chair back.

'Maggie, last summer I wrote to you that I wanted to tell you something about myself.'

'Yes.'

Maggie put her hand on the back of Katherine's chair. She was beside, but behind her, neither could see the other's face.

'Have you ever thought what that was?'

'I know what it might be.'

'I want very much to tell you.'

'I think I wrote back then in a timid selfish way; now all is different; I fear nothing, tell me everything you want to.'

'I think you know.'

'Yes.'

Another long silence. A slight coldness, like a grey cloud is creeping into Maggie's mind, but her heart glows. She puts her palm upon the bent back before her.

'Don't be afraid of me, Kathy, tell me all you want to and only what you want to.'

Another silence. One of the hands goes down and picks up a

crust of bread, crumbling it, The voice changes, becoming lighter.

'All the same it is very hard to tell now I come to the point.'

And then, helped by the intuition between them and by guessing and questioning as they go, Katherine tells. Tells that she has learned what Love is.

'And I have never regretted it, not for a moment. I have no regret, no remorse.'

And she looks round now with a perfect smile; a smile so wonderful in brilliant understanding and quiet content that Maggie sees there indeed is life, not abuse of it – love, not playing with it: truth, not any fear of life.

'Ask me any questions you like. Haven't you wondered at my relations with Todia?'

'*Kathy*! I thought you were another person with him than I had ever seen you before, but I have wondered about nothing. I should have said this were impossible.'

'It is so simple, so natural; so simple, so natural, Mag.' And again there is that marvellous smile, a grave smile.

'And it was so long ago as three years?' asked Maggie, wondering.

'Yes.'

Maggie thought: Now you cannot go to the sea with Pierre; you cannot fulfil your love for Pierre. Maggie held her breath to listen. Who had spoken? It was nothing. An inconsequent idea that had floated through her throbbing brain; but she gave her trouble in words.

'A slight coldness, like a grey cloud' has crept into Maggie's mind. This cloud then blackens: she realises that she cannot now go away with Pierre as she meant to. This would be comprehensible if the 'grey' or black cloud threatened *after* Violet said that she had been Pierre's lover, but why now? Is Margaret experiencing an intimation that she would become like Violet (a free woman), if she went away with Pierre? It is understandable she would not want to be teamed with her sister as a bohemian.

Besides the 'grey cloud' here, there is also metaphorically a light that flickers in this part of the story, one which later becomes incandescent and is brightest in a letter which Margaret wrote to Violet after her confession was over. This is the light of the ideal Katherine/Violet, the other sister who in Margaret's mind is progressively glamorised, even sanctified, a sister fast becoming an icon with a

perfect smile; a smile so wonderful in brilliant understanding and quiet content that Maggie sees there indeed is life, not abuse of it – love, not playing with it: truth, not any fear of life.

But this is to anticipate: the transformation or sanctification of Violet is yet to come. Before this flicker becomes a flame, the grey cloud turns to black. Margaret is getting frightened and has to interrogate Katherine/Violet.

'All this in you has nothing to do with me and yet since you have told me, I feel that I can't go away with Pierre.'

Katherine was silent, and Maggie continued her slow questioning. They had talked a few moments about Maggie's new decision. On her side, as if she spoke of a stranger, Kathy had introduced the subject.

She said, 'I have wanted to tell you all this so much, oh, so much, but till tonight it has seemed impossible.' . . .

'He told you I had promised to go away with him?'

'I wished directly you had gone. I told him you were free to hear anything he wished to say of me.'

'Yes, I have promised, and of course I know what it will mean.'

And Katherine repeated, 'Ask me anything. I *want* to tell you.'

'I have nothing more to ask. I think I understand, Kathy, only it is all so new. I have never believed it. Aunty Rosalie told me she was sure of it, I said I *knew* it was not so.

'You remember the poet, Max Voloshinov. He was another.'

'How can one love two men?' puzzled Maggie. Her brain felt numb, and yet it was a whirl of thoughts.

There was a knock at the door.

The sisters are then interrupted. Violet has a visitor, Krouglikoff.

Katherine looked annoyed and defiant: another knock: then slowly she went to the door. It was Krouglikoff. She entered, full of spirit. Kindly words for Maggie came first, then enquiries after Katherine's work. The sisters sat looking at her, Maggie blankly, Katherine with that thin pained look that always flew into her gaze when, as a child, she suffered morally. They hardly spoke, unable to answer her questions except by monosyllables.

She stayed for an hour and was at her best: sympathetic, gentle, bright. By a great effort Maggie regained some presence of mind and chattered haltingly. Katherine sat with her splendid head drooped on to one hand, shading her face from the lamp light. Krouglikoff spoke of Max and Todia. When at ten o'clock Krouglikoff left them the sisters stood neither looking at the other, each feeling constraint, each straining to re-touch the point of interruption, and so continue that which once started could not be left in suspension. They moved about putting away the supper things seeking for an opportunity. Maggie thought Katherine over-tired, needing sleep – always an imperative need for her – and suggested it, but Katherine said with a note of intensity in her voice that they must still talk.

So they undressed. Katherine got into bed and Maggie in her dressing gown sat at the foot of the bed. The lamp was put out.

Katherine started again opening herself to all the wonder, ignorance and curiosity Maggie could express. They talked for several hours. Gradually and very gently the younger sister showed to the stunned, bewildered Maggie her point of view. Love for her was not, so Maggie gathered, a single passion awakened by only one man, but a compound thing given to several, even the point of actual union, and then followed by separation, complete even to the point of losing sight of each other.

'But one keeps always a very true, a warm, affection for him. Cold calculation. *No!* never that.'

For to Maggie it seemed so difficult to accept at the same time absence of love in her sense and necessary presence of love in Katherine's. Patiently, Katherine tried to explain her life and her view of life. She spoke of love, of what love was to her and those with whom she lived, of the immense gain it had been to her. She told how that when the greatest hour of Nature was lived, all other hours were lived more richly, that [once the] most wonderful part of life [was] known, all life became more clear.

Then they talked long of the question of the prevention of children.

They were a long while silent waiting till a fresh puzzle should present itself to Maggie's mind, but she was dreamily listening to that same voice which had repeated that now things were changed with regard to herself and Pierre. She felt so tired, but wanted still to strive to reach Katherine's point of view. Affection and sympathy must carry her over years of experience in an hour and place her, knowing all things now, by her sister's side, where but a few hours ago she had been ignorant of this greatest experience of Katherine's life.

Suddenly her heart felt sick and she seemed to stop breathing. An idea so frightful that she dared not face it had come suddenly from the darkness and placed itself before her. 'No, no.' It was impossible. A horrible, horrible thought, she would not admit, but there it was, it gripped her. She began to feel frightened.

She must know.

She could not think. She tried to reassure herself by thinking of the past, by reason, but her whole being answered to no appeal, but the sense of the horrible Something bearing down upon her. It grew and grew.

'Ask me anything you like, dear old Meg.'

The voice came from far off. Nearer and nearer came the ghastly Thing.

'Even personal questions?' asked Maggie then. Her lips were dry, she spoke with difficulty, sitting up to get more breath.

'Yes,' hesitatingly.

Silence.

She cannot ask: she will never so wrong her sister. For shame to harbour such a thought for a moment.

Ah! God! It is on me. It has me!

I must know, I must know: I must know!

'Katherine!' Her voice is so strange she cannot recognise it.

'You said – there were – three.'

A long pause.

'Who was the third?'

'But Maggie, you know! (The first, you mean.) You *must* know.'

'No, I don't know.'

'Him, surely?'

Katherine's voice is full of pain, of frightened foreboding, but Maggie speaks on, slowly in the same low voice; nothing could stop her now, not entreaties, nothing could stop her and she asks again.

'You said there were three. I *don't* know. Max – and Todia – and – the third?'

That awful shade which five minutes before was unknown to her is becoming the only reality in her life.

'You don't know?'

'No.'

'Then I can't tell you,' whispered Katherine.

There is dead stillness.

Slowly Maggie reaches out her hand on the blankets before her and leans forward over it, crouching, toward Katherine's face, her chin thrust stiffly out, her eyes wide and still. The room is dark. She can hardly speak. Her lips are starched and dry. One word falls down and a dead leaf rustles and drops on Katherine's straining ears.

'*Pierre?*'

'Yes'

Silence.

'But Maggie, Maggie, I thought you knew from the beginning!'

'No.'

And Katherine sees that in all her life she will never hear a more bitter wail than that word: she does not speak. There is a long silence. The face on the pillow is full of anguish; her heart yearns toward her sister. She feels she would give her own happiness to change this bitterness.

At last she hears Maggie's teeth chattering.

'You had better get into bed,' she whispers.

No movement. Again, several times, with silence between them, the teeth chatter, they chatter violently and with a loose hard sound as though they were a death's head's teeth.

'Meg, do get into bed.'

Then in the dim light Katherine sees her slowly rise, stagger, try to recover herself, and fall across her own bed. The teeth are chattering horribly now. The whole frame is shaken by convulsive shuddering. For an hour Katherine tended the wretched girl, rubbing her icy feet and hands, sitting still beside her, heating water for a hot-water bottle, and milk, that could not be drunk. Alternately Maggie lay quite still and was violently convulsed and then again the shivering and the chattering teeth against which she fought in vain, sitting up and holding her face fiercely in both hands.

'I am all right, Kathy, quite all right,' she had repeated over and over again in a forced dreadful voice of cheerfulness immediately after falling, and she could say nothing but that. Now she was silent, and when much later, after Katherine had gone back to bed, she asked Maggie anxiously a question, the poor child only managed to moan faintly 'I – can't – talk – tonight' and then sighed as after an immense effort. She lay on her back with either arm at her side stunned and exhausted.

In the three or four moments that had followed Katherine's 'Yes', Maggie had sat as still, as passive as a thing of stone, and back on to her had rushed with violence all the love given and received, the promise of the future, the joy, the hope, the love of the future. Her heart seemed to stand still with wide open doors while all that it had put forth, all that had made life worth living to her rushed, crowded into the doors leaving the world empty and the heart suffered anguish. Maggie had felt this pain growing so violent that it seemed to be crushing out life itself. And still the backwards flood continued. Everything fell from life, hurling itself, destroyed, into her. Soon she realized that she was actually losing her vitality, but still she sat, the recipient, for destruction of all her life's worth. At last, she thought of moving. She could not. She could not find her body. Then the shivering had seized her. Still she did not stir. It was only Katherine's repeated words that brought her again within call of her senses and material things. Now as she lay there, all was over, all was finished: life had died, for love was dead.

All that she had was destroyed by her sister, by that one word: 'Yes.'

Margaret's story stops here. She did not write down what happened next, but we do know from Pierre's journal that she sent him a note by a messenger and that she did see him before she left Paris, and that she told him she loved him, and he remembered the years of loving her and the *citron pressé* moment (himself, Margaret and Mrs Court squeezed together in icy Switzerland) and he wrote that she had become beautiful and that he had 'become good'. We know what happened next from a letter to Pierre which Margaret began on Friday 23 March and finished the next morning, an hour before she left for Gare du Nord. Much of this she wrote while 'Violet is asleep – and she keeps moaning. How I hate leaving her tomorrow' and 'now I must get up and dress and go back to England'. Pierre thought Margaret's letters had a 'Shakespearean' quality. He may have meant their driving momentum.

Margaret first writes about how everything is changed by Violet's confession. A year before there had been the 'kiss of

leave-taking' in Paris, in the 'wretched condition' of not knowing if she loved him. 'All is clear' now, a clarity which evolves in
the course of her letter. There were stages in the horror.

> I learned that Violet had once given herself to you, which to
> me, then, following on the talk we had, hard and judging,
> somewhat in the dark, meant that somewhat lightly, although
> having affection for you, she had allowed you to teach her
> what love was, and, from you had passed on to men she cared
> more for than for you. (Burn this letter when you have read
> it.)

A critical sentence now follows: 'Instantly I saw that, for a
comparatively light and calculated reason Violet had stolen from
me the sweetness and richness of life for which I had so long
waited and so intensely longed.'

> I saw you cut away from me just as I was going into your arms
> – I saw black night come all round me just as I seemed to be
> passing from shadow into light. Well, all that was false.

Margaret is bereaved literally, that is, 'robbed' and, she fears,
robbed 'somewhat lightly'. She had known Pierre's theories
about love ever since their talks in Paris in 1899. Now she
knows Violet is a convert to them, educated surely by Pierre, and
in this state Violet had taken Pierre from her. But at this stage, in
a psychological move either advanced by her own drives or by
what Violet said to her on the Thursday or Friday before
departure, Margaret's horrified sense of bereavement is changed
into another state and a strange one: a state of exultation in
suffering which is also an exaltation of Violet.

> Now there is neither horror nor bitterness, but only full and
> satisfied acceptance of things as they are. For you see, when
> Violet thought I had understood what she had to tell I did not
> at all get the truth of it, but something else. The shock was so
> great, the repulse to my own feelings so violent that, strong as I

am, it affected me physically to the point of making me helpless for a while.

But only for a while. The next thought in the letter is that Violet *did* love Pierre and always had done. Did Violet say things that made Margaret believe this after her confession of the plain facts? It is possible because Margaret wrote in her letter that the sense of betrayal 'of the hours before Violet talked to me this evening are non-existent now'. This could be what was said on Thursday or Friday. It is hard to believe that Violet admitted to a love for Pierre that excluded Margaret. She believed what she said about free unions, however frequently she was needy for Pierre. What happened was that, just as Margaret devised a new name for Violet in her story (not for herself, nor Pierre, nor Krouglikoff), so she re-wrote Violet's character, and devised a great love for her, a love which flooded the space she longed to occupy.

Now I know that Violet loves you. Everything is changed. I not only accept things as they are, but I am content with things as they are. Everything is changed for me. How good it is in the light at last, and there are no screens between one's eyes and the truth.

Pierre, I have never known Violet. How unspeakably I have undervalued her character. I thought I loved her devotingly and admired her character, yet this wonderful part of her, with its flooding richness and its unshakeable strength was unknown to me.

So Violet loved you before I did. Violet, saying not a word, gave up her chance because she saw – but I feel I have no right to talk about it, although you know it all.

I am so glad, I am so thankful she has told me. Of course I ought to have known. Always I have expected it, always remembered that it was possible, yet only egoism has blinded me to it, all these years and to such an extent.

I need not say, need I, that all the feelings of the hours before Violet talked to me this evening are non-existent now? Some are reversed, as for instance, the feeling that Violet had taken you from me is now changed to the knowledge that she, in a sense, she herself, that is, gave you to me, long ago, and without talking. I used to think that Violet must love you in the old days in Conway, Switzerland, but I was deceived by her freedom and boyishness. Here complete affection blinded me. Then it got to separation and it seemed to me that Violet's beauty of body and soul were such that you *must* learn to love her and it was the realization of this possibility alone that kept me from confessing to Violet my love for you through the wretched loneliness of separation. I think you would realise this pretty strongly if you were ever to read my diary. I remember the feeling and the suffering of not being able to tell her, tho' perhaps I didn't write much about it. I told myself that Violet must never know I loved you, and if you and she were to love one another this knowledge would be a great unhappiness and make life harder and less simple. Then, last Easter in Paris, when I found that you did love me still, the possibility of love between you and Violet seemed at an end and I told her, breaking down the barrier. Since then for a year we have not lived within sight of each other. Now we are together.

Pierre, Pierre don't you see that it is impossible now that I should give myself to you? Violet feels as I do. Her desire for my happiness, her wish that she should not stand between me and you, these other considerations are additional, external, different from the real pure *instinct* of the thing; and surely with regard to this, the centre or essence as it were of nature, one's ideas should be based, not on voluntary thought, but on involuntary, primeval deepest feeling? I am so glad Violet feels as I do: but it could not be otherwise as she loves you. Please do not think I mean that Violet would deter me from giving myself to you – on the contrary, she would urge me to act as if she did not exist in the case, but this attitude is, as I said, arrived at by learning, by unselfishness, by willingness to give to sacrifice, *is* not THE TRUE, the true, the natural attitude and Violet admits it. The thing is impossible.

When I use the word impossible I do not mean 'I ought not, dare not, may not or cannot'. I mean it is the same as when one says it is impossible to fly to the moon, to walk through a rock, to turn a rose into a fir tree. Simply, the thing does not exist.

Try, Pierre, to imagine the situation. Violet loving you deeply, taking and giving with you, and I loving you as passionately, if not as well, and you taking now one and now the other, and of the love between Violet and me? Our thoughts of each other? The yearning of the one torturing her with hunger while the other she knew was being satisfied. You have never had a brother or sister. You cannot perhaps realise, even by strong effort to do so, what sisterhood at its strongest can be, what it must be, even where it is not, as with us, intensely strong. You see, it would be difficult enough if we were only friends.

In the margin Margaret wrote: '*Of course* I don't mean jealousy. I think that is in neither of us.'

Margaret's passion to annihilate herself out of her love, and virtually to bestow it on Violet, gathers momentum and becomes mythically empowered. 'Is it Celtic blood which brings its traces of superstition and the worship of Nature? I don't know.' Margaret seems to realise that her situation has potential for self-dramatisation. 'Please don't think I am writing like this to smooth things over and patch a broken affair. Not for a moment. I am writing as truthfully as I can, what I feel at the time of writing; and far from thinking anything needs smoothing or mending. Just now I can say with you, Pierre, 'I like whatever happens.' (The quotation is one from Nietzsche that Pierre had sent to her.)

As she came to her last minutes in Paris, whether out of fatigue or maturity, Margaret ends with a refreshingly plain reflection:

Now I must get up and dress and go back to England. To find that Violet and I love one man, well it is to find an extraordinary link, to find union where there was always proximity, that is all.

Violet continued to dwell as before in Montparnassian bohemia. Krouglikoff had a party lit by Chinese lanterns. She was dressed as Napoleon and Violet went as a boy. Violet was reading Herbert Spencer and Dostoyevsky. In May 1907, a month or so after her confession to Margaret, she went back to Kingsnorth for Easter.

She had been distressed by the night of confession. She wrote to Pierre, now in Munich, that they (really she) should have been frank earlier. When Margaret wrote to her after her sudden departure for home she seemed to be bearing up, but she had always been capable of writing with resolution. Face to face she was alarmingly hectic, doing more housework than was necessary, and – irritatingly – she would not leave Violet alone. 'She loves me too much,' she wrote to Pierre. In her solitary, sometimes phlegmatic way, Violet felt she could not return as much as Margaret emotionally delivered. In a letter to Pierre, Margaret wrote how beautiful Violet looked when she was asleep: she wanted to stroke ('éffleurer') her neck. Pierre remembered he once asked Violet whether she could caress Margaret a little. They both loved him, he thought, and wondered whether he would want them to be 'lesbiennes'. 'Violet thought about it, too.' Pierre thought of asking Violet 'to help her yourself', as he wrote in a note in English on one of Violet's letters. She thought she could not do anything premeditated because she was not a physical person, except with lovers. She found it disagreeable to embrace Margaret who had always been the more outgoing girl. As Violet wrote this, Margaret was dancing to barrel-organ music in the Courts' garden. As time passed they ceased to get on each other's nerves. Margaret once asked plaintively if Violet thought it was still too late to be Pierre's sister. Violet thought the difference between them was Margaret would never recover from Pierre, but that she could, though the thought of his intimacy was irresistible when she did not have another lover – indeed, it was a compelling thought when she *did* have a lover. She wrote to Pierre that in Paris, 'it will be hard to stay away from you. The more love I have, the more I need.' She wanted to remove herself from the space into which she had been forced, it seemed, between Pierre and Margaret. (Had this desire driven her to confess to Margaret in the first place? By explicitly placing herself between them, had she tried to remove herself from the imaginary space she had occupied, into which they had, severally, placed her?) Violet went up to London a few times and saw Shaw's *Don Juan in Hell* and Wilde's *A Woman of No Importance*, significant titles considering the sisters' experience. They did not talk about either play, but conversation was easing. In June Violet managed to ask Margaret about her confession of 'Solitary Vice'. Margaret said it did not happen so often now and felt less guilt-ridden because she realised that it was tiredness which brought it on. It did not really please her very much, except sometimes when she woke up. The sisters went to a fortune-teller who said that Margaret would never be happy in love. Obviously Violet was glad to get back to Paris in early July 1907 and we will see how soon she went much further afield.

Margaret was left alone with Mother and Stephen in Kingsnorth. Although she did some work at St Jude's in Whitechapel, she left the village only rarely and she did not contact Pierre again for a year and a half. Then at Christmas 1908 she wrote to Pierre to say she wanted to see him. She did so. Chapter XX of *Two English Girls and the Continent*, entitled 'The Three Days', describes a meeting when they actually stayed together. Like all chapters in the novel there is a date at the head of it, in this case 'Paris. 15 Avril 1909'. However, it is likely that Margaret visited Pierre in Paris *twice* in 1909 and also likely that neither visit was in April. From her letters (of which many survive about this phase) Margaret probably went to Paris early in 1909, spending evenings with Pierre, but not nights, and the days with a girl-friend. She wrote later that 'I ought to have had a perfectly free time to think and dream and feel all day. But it was the best we could get, and what a good best, too.' At last she felt close to Pierre, and afterwards sometimes referred to his Alésia apartment as home. The 'Three Days' described in Chapter XX actually occurred late in November 1909. It was during this visit that they at last had sex together. We can be sure of this because we have Margaret's letters of late 1909 to early

1910 in which she wonders if her period will come and notes when it did.

While Margaret was planning her visit to Paris in early 1909 and Pierre was expecting her, he wrote in his journal that he was 'working over' her letters and thinking about her 'variableness'. He had been reading Otto Weininger's *Sex and Character* (1906), which deeply impressed him with its picture of the fluctuating or 'totally sexual' nature of women, a picture with which Pierre himself identified, seeing himself as a 'feminine' person. Women, said Weininger, were psychologically supple, devious, and self-accusatory: they played their cards with 'impudence', graciously but always sincerely, with an evolving ingenuity that was frightening. Pierre thought that he, too, possessed a kind of 'hysteria', as he called it. He once said women liked him because they saw how much courage he had to summon up to woo them. Margaret had always frightened him and now he was to see her without interruption, and he knew she was to see him with full knowledge of his love-affairs, including his relationship with Violet. They had a friendly time in Paris in early 1909, but when Margaret returned she sent letters to Pierre which show that the visit was 'of great moral importance'. Now she felt as if she were 'severed from my old life, cut off from my old place.' She threw herself into neighbourhood farm work, on one letter inking a tiny sketch of herself on a wet day in February in a below-the-knee Holland overall, blue serge hood and her Paris sabots, with Dash her dog, cats and chickens. In the background there is a minuscule Stephen ('Farmer Court is standing still so it must be Sunday') and two peacocks. Margaret was often vivacious, but she was not cheerful, still not knowing what place Pierre had in her life. Once she refers to her 'maidenhead', implying he has taken it though he had not – but she was so engaged with him he might as well have done. She wrote out for him a dream which she had soon after returning from Paris. She was sitting at a little square table with Pierre, surely at Alésia, by the fire, his back to her, 'thankful of the silence and for his averted face'. She 'looked and looked.'

You had the form of a woman, dark brown hair and black silk dress, but outward form is nothing. It was Pierre. I leaned forward irresistibly and slipped my left hand down into yours. Then the silence no longer satisfied you and you asked me what I meant, persistently. I did not know. I struggled for words but my lips clung together. Suddenly they parted in a startled exclamation and with a jump I woke.

She still thought rather strangely that she 'had to be loyal to Violet'. Interestingly Pierre appears as female, a sign that he/she was not threatening. He had told her about how he identified with woman as described by Weininger. It was now, after her first visit of 1909, that Margaret sent to Pierre her diaries. He thought they were 'almost a finished work in itself'. Margaret wondered if they could meet again, in Rouen or at the Alésia apartment, and her mother picked up the wish. 'I think it is a *great* pity to open that connection – it will be thought that you are putting yourself forward again.' But Margaret did go, and the events described in 'The Three Days' and Roché's notes took place.

On 17 November 1909 Margaret arrived at the Gare du Nord just before six o'clock. Pierre thought that she looked somewhat 'rural'. She had two bags, in one of which she carried a loaf of bread baked by herself. Pierre sniffed the offering appreciatively and Margaret showed him a snapshot of herself and Dash. A newspaper cutting fell out of her bag, with a quotation from Tolstoy on it: 'So long as there are children of the poor and needy in the world, the duty of a Christian is to take care of them and not create any others.' After all this time he recognised the 'gaiety' of Margaret's features. Their 'belle camaraderie' to-gether immediately resumed. The mobility of Margaret's face was something Pierre often mentioned.

The couple took the Métro to Alésia. After being shown around Margaret asked Pierre what he had been doing. He said he had been writing a magazine article, so she told him to go on with it and he did so for an hour. It was now the end of the evening and they went to separate beds, but then because it was so cold, they did lie down together, both in pyjamas. Outside, and some of the time inside, it was freezing. The next day, while shopping and cooking, they talked and talked, remembering their first meetings when the Court family stayed in Paris. Pierre gave an example of English prudishness which in his novel he attributed to Anne: how a girl was shocked when a boy raised the skirt of a wooden doll. They talked about sex and Pilar. Pierre said that Pilar was his Clarisse (that is, Margaret's nine-year-old cousin from whom she learned sexual sensations and 'Solitary Vice'). 'If only there hadn't been a cousin,' said Muriel. 'There is always a cousin,' Pierre retorted with French sagacity. Pierre wrote in his journal that Margaret was still 'Sparta'. 'A beach of fine, warm sand with a little sea-shell. A well of lyres.' On the third night they took off their pyjamas in bed and were completely at ease. 'I turned her gently towards me, with a new joy. I put her face against my shoulder, my hand tentatively against the bush of her sex. My finger went further down, pushed softly, moved in a little and felt the neatness and elasticity of her virginity. I realised my 'petit homme' had woken up and was ready. While the end of my finger was still wanting to touch her virginity, my penis urged me to press against Nuk, moving forward to seek a way in. It moved, eager for steadiness, made the break and then was inside. Nuk was completely still. The hymen gave way more easily than Violet's. Margaret's eyes were open. I looked to see if I was really in, and, yes, there was a red line traced round the root of my penis, and some blood spreading. Blood, whiteness and redness. It looked beautiful.' 'I am your wife now,' said Margaret.

Afterwards Margaret warmed her feet by the fire and Pierre noticed that her toes were flexible and widely spaced, with rather square nails. Always the 'informateur', Pierre wondered about how she felt when his finger was inside her. Was it the same as when she touched herself? Roché wrote down that he was enchanted by Violet and Pilar, but he had wanted to discover everything with Margaret. On the last page of his journal entry about their three days together, he wrote, 'No sensual pleasure. Nothing but love.'

Margaret returned to England, wondering whether she would be pregnant, indeed hoping for a baby. She had a worry: if she were pregnant, would a child be 'defective' because she 'didn't take my share' when they made love? 'I was so calm. My mind wasn't turned towards the child, nor toward thee lovingly.' (After her recovery from blindness Margaret often used 'thee' to Pierre.) As a lover Margaret had been the opposite of Violet, or the opposite of the lover Violet became. She had been remote, peacefully gazing past Pierre, probably without orgasm. (Taking 'my share' may have been a reference to orgasm: she may have had in mind the traditional Victorian belief that female orgasm increased the likelihood of conception.) In any case, her experience of becoming Pierre's lover was not threatening.

Back in England, she still could refer to Pierre as a 'god', but with reference to the past, to her long-standing and still-surviving obsession. When she wrote she was now more resolute in dismissing his values: 'It was a terrible thing to take the virginity of a woman who has old-fashioned ideas about wifehood and motherhood,' but she hastens to add that 'she gave it rather than he took it'. She is now also an affectionate writer to the man who seems to have become physically smaller and sweeter after the three days. 'Cuddle me, please. Fold your arms closely around me. Let me nestle my face beneath yours, now I can whisper to you.'

What of Violet in the months before Margaret's three days with Pierre?

When Violet left Kingsnorth in the summer of 1907 she went much further afield than Paris. An event had occurred which changed her future and the overladen relationships within the trio, one which finally removed her from the space between Pierre and Margaret.

For some time Violet had been haplessly trying to contact Max Voloshinov who had disappeared into Russia. She had received some addresses for him from Pierre and written, but no replies had arrived. While she was at Kingsnorth in May 1907 a letter from him was at last forwarded to her. Max invited her to visit him for the months of August and September in a house in the Caucasus. His wife would be living nearby, and so would his mother. Violet instantly decided to accept the invitation, rent out her attic in Paris and, after staying in Georgia, go on to Moscow and St Petersburg where she could meet many of her Café Russe friends, whether or not things worked out with Max. She would call on Pierre in Paris. The invitation meant a reunion with all things Russian. Her fate lay in Russia now.

Violet lived in the Voloshinov ménage. She liked his patient wife and his mother. She had always enjoyed sea-bathing, and preferred it in the hot Caucasus, with the backdrop of mountains, beautifully painted in Max's watercolours, than on the south coast of Cornwall where the Courts liked to camp. It was soon evident that her affair with Max was over. She moved on to St Petersburg where she met Vladimir or 'Volodia' whom she had helped in Paris to learn French. Volodia had experimented as a painter, but was now working as a forestry officer in the Russian civil service. He hated desk work and, at about the time Violet arrived, an opportunity arose for him to do practical work as a master-forester in Siberia. But he fell suddenly and violently in love with Violet, and they lived together for a month in Lesnoy in early 1908. She was taken aback by his unqualified delight in her, so different from the planned concerns of her other two major lovers, Pierre and Max, both of whom were cultural missionaries with a cause, who had frequently explained commitments, journeys, excuses, acolytes, and special, frequently articulated moralities. Volodia was ready to throw in his lot with Violet and she was even fascinated by the idea of living with him in Siberia. She loved the way he sang operatic arias and folk-songs, proud of his peasant ancestry, in a beautiful light baritone. He was vulnerably sad. 'His melancholy is my master – and he, so simple: I love him.' For Pierre, it was Margaret who was the 'Great North', but of the two sisters it was Violet who lived through the metaphor. It was she who had written passionately to Pierre, longing for an erotic solitude in the icy tracts of Norway and now she was prepared to go to the Siberian fastnesses with Volodia. But whether she was ready to marry, as Volodia wanted, was a problem, as was his carnal jealousy. She was eventually persuaded.

On 14 September 1908, Violet and Volodia were married. Violet was still nervous of being tied to a man with high sensitivity to her moods, with a jealousy-driven access to her inner thoughts. He said he would kill himself if she was interested in someone else. 'Sometimes I think that my past was better than my future will be,' Violet wrote to Pierre. Volodia suffered because he knew that she was not sure of marriage, and was suspicious of Pierre, whom he only knew from afar. All of which was suddenly forgotten when Violet caught typhus and desperately needed Margaret to nurse her. In November 1908 Margaret went to St Petersburg to stay with them for five weeks. She seemed to Violet more religious than ever and not interested at all in the art and music that could be seen and heard in the capital. How could she be interested with no Russian and a sick sister? Luckily Violet soon recovered, and Margaret returned to England. Violet's illness was immediately followed by pregnancy. In May 1909 she and Volodia went to England, back to the security of the Court household and Margaret's help again.

In June 1909 Nicholas Vladimirovich was born. By now Volodia had decided against a career in forestry. He was intent on becoming a full-time artist, and had to depend to some degree on Violet's income. Life was not easy for Violet and Volodia who finally decided to settle in England, though Paris beckoned. By the end of 1919, they had had two more children, Oleg and Tatiana. As well as being a talented painter, Volodia had some training in stage design (from Léon Bakst in Russia), and both he and Violet were able to work as designers and scene painters for various inter-continental and British companies. Volodia wrote quite an important book on stage design and after the war taught at a leading London art school. Throughout her life Violet painted and, was particularly in demand for portraits.

Almost from the time Margaret first met Pierre in 1899, she had known another man. She had met Tom Garnett while doing social work at the girls' hostel in Drury Lane. Garnett was a clerical official with the Royal Mail in London. He worked for girls' clubs in his spare time and was also an active member of a progressive organisation in Finsbury called the South Place Ethical Society, which was frequented by social workers and 'Toynbeeites'. The history of South Place went back to the late eighteenth century when it began as a Universalist congregation whose Christian faith was even less doctrinally orthodox than that of the Unitarians. It had a plain chapel in Finsbury and in the course of the nineteenth century it changed its name to the South Place Religious Society, becoming a humanistic, agnostic body which organised itself with Sunday 'services', but whose hymns were dedicated more to progress and mankind than to any orthodoxy deity or supernatural being. In Tom's and Margaret's time its object was stated to be 'The cultivation of a rational religious sentiment, the study of ethical principles and the promotion of human welfare in harmony with existing knowledge.' In 1887 its name was changed to the South Place Ethical Society at the insistence of its new American leader (not minister), Stanton Coit. He set up a small but tenacious network of similar societies, combining charitable work with classes in philosophy. Ethicists were rationalists but, unlike secularists, they wanted to affirm a spiritual dimension in life, considering themselves to be 'constructive rationalists'. 'We find that almost every day we are approaching the borders of a realm of thought, reason and experiment in which the subtler unseen forces of physical nature are more and more coming into play.' Later South Place Ethical Society moved to its own building, which still stands, a humanist centre called Conway Hall, in the corner of Red Lion Square in London.

Tom Garnett was an active ethicist and, like Pierre Roché, a great traveller. Margaret had never been seriously attracted to him in the years of thinking about Pierre and after the three days she felt secretly married to Pierre. In 1909 Tom asked whether he could correspond with her, perhaps hoping for an understanding. She tried to explain to him that she could not marry because she was in some sense another's, even managing to say to him that she had lost her virginity when it seemed that he could not understand her scruples. He comforted her, after tramping around London streets. Hardly anyone had put their arms around her, which he did, a 'gentle, splendid friend'. 'I do love him very much as a sort of great big much older brother,' Margaret wrote to Pierre. Her letters seek reasons for not accepting Tom so fluently that it seems as if she instinctively does not want him: or if she does want him, and cannot have him, it is not because she is no longer a virgin, nor because she is Pierre's wife and marriage would therefore be adultery, but because she feels herself to be an adulterer in a more subtle sense. By becoming Pierre's lover she had joined the party of adulterers, those who disdained marriage. She became, though she would never say it, a Violet, who provided, as brothers and sisters do, the sort of rôle-repellent envied by only children who have to make solitary experiments with being the sort of people they decide eventually not to be.

As war approached there occurred one of those structural changes in family life which prove a catalyst for change. Stephen Court met an Irish girl whom he wanted to marry. Now there was one less person for Margaret to look after, or one more to help look after Mother. Even Mrs Court said that Margaret did not need be at home so much, but when Margaret said she wanted to go to training college to become a teacher, 'the family were dead set against it'. Mother always came first. Margaret agreed to drop the idea and take a tour of Belgium instead, after Stephen's wedding. Margaret's sight was still poor, but she had discovered an American Christian healer, Dr Mills, who excited her, seemed to do good and who paid occasional visits to London. She even asked Pierre to come over to attend one of his public healing services; not surprisingly, he did not. In April 1913 Margaret travelled with her mother to Stephen's wedding in Ireland, going by way of Conway in north Wales, where she remembered the trio's beach walks and the yellow gorse behind their cottage. Afterwards there was a spring holiday in Brittany with Violet and Volodia; Nicholas played in the white sand with shells and cuttlefish. Margaret let Pierre know where they were. On their return to England, she wrote to Tom who had been on a walking tour in Poland. She had realised suddenly that it was time to move on, and, as Pierre (*via* Nietzsche) had told her, it was time to accept whatever is given. She wrote to Pierre that she was wrong to have refused to let Tom woo her and that in the last three years love between them 'had been growing root downward, deep and slow'. On a Saturday morning at the beginning of October, having been reading, 'entrancedly', Rabindranath Tagore, she made up her mind. She decided to have a husband in Tom and Pierre could have 'The Work'.

Tom Garnett and Margaret Court decided to be married soon at St Jude's in Whitechapel, the old church of Samuel Barnett, founder of Toynbee Hall. First, Margaret wrote to Pierre to say good-bye.

> Your life, with those other women, makes me shudder still, though I unwaveringly tell myself *you* believe you are right. But to me it is wrong and abhorrent, and that grows stronger in me and would separate us even if this love for my own husband did not separate us. I want to meet you only in God, in prayer – *never* in actuality.
>
> Good bye. God guard you.
>
> M.
>
> Answer to arrive no later than Monday. Then we go to Greece *via* Rheims and Basle.

In 1914 her daughter, christened Margaret, was born. It has never been common in England to give a daughter her mother's name.

The wedding was only a few months before the First World War. Not many years after the end of which Margaret was to die, while Violet lived on until 1950. In 1914 Pierre was established in another trio, partnering himself with Franz Hessel and Helen Grund. Margaret and Violet had receded into his past. We will see how they revisited Pierre in spirit, when news came of them about a decade later and how thirty years later still Henri Pierre Roché decided to make a novel out of the experience of his first loves, the novel which, in turn, was to haunt François Truffaut.

In the next two chapters we shall move away from the English girls to see what happened to Roché and how Truffaut joined their story.

Chapter Four

henri pierre roché: the man who loved

Gertrude Stein did not always like Henri Pierre Roché and described him drily in her odd style. This man, she wrote

> is certainly loving, doing a good deal of loving, certainly this one has been completely excited by such a thing. Certainly this one has been completely dreaming about such a thing. Certainly this one is one who would be very pleasant to very many in loving.

Loving was part of 'The Work' for Roché who said in 1919 that he wanted 'to write the story of my life one day like Casanova, but in a different spirit.' He was indeed like Casanova as described by his British fellow free spirit, Havelock Ellis. In 1898 Ellis wrote that the famous lover

> fully grasped what the scientific psychology of sex calls the secondary law of courting, namely the development in the male of an imaginative attentiveness to the psychical and bodily states of the female, in place of an exclusive attentiveness to his own gratification. It is not impossible that in these matters Casanova could have given a lesson to many virtuous husbands of our own highly moral century. He never sank to the level of the vulgar maxim that all's fair in love and war.

Roché did cause great pain, but neither would he have subscribed to that banal maxim.

By 1914 Roché had begun to live according to the pattern which marked his life. His career is somewhat hard to epitomise, though its outline and nature will eventually become clearer when more of his writings, including the journals, are published. Always excepting *Jules and Jim*, kept faithfully in print by Gallimard along with the less popular *Two English Girls and the Continent*, hardly any of Roché's writings have been reprinted and studies of his life have only recently started to emerge. The first fund of information about him was the exhibition catalogue by Carlton Lake and Linda Ashton called *Henri Pierre: An Introduction* and a chapter in Lake's *Confessions of a Literary Archaeologist* at the beginning of which Roché is succinctly characterised.* He spent his life, said Lake, in three principal ways:

> (1) making friends, (2) being a kind of private art dealer (guiding people like John Quinn, Hilla Rebay, and other affluent collectors who benefited from his judgment and connections), and (3) keeping a journal. Transcribed single-spaced on 8″ by 11″ sheets, his journal runs to about seven thousand pages. Among other things it established two facts: (1) Roché was, without any doubt, one of the greatest lovers in the history of literature, and (2) he documented that aspect of his life in such a thoroughgoing and convincing manner as to make him – in the judgment of the few who have read even some portions of his unpublished journal – one of the greatest diarists in the history of love.

Lake was right as far as he went, but left out the fact that Roché was also a writer on art, and a novelist, though he only became one late in life, publishing *Jules and Jim* in 1953 and *Two English Girls and the Continent* in 1956. When he died in April 1959 he was at work on a novel called *Victor*, based on his friendship with Marcel Duchamp. A draft was posthumously

* Ashton and Lake's *Introduction* is effectively a 'study', or an unconventional biography, not a mere catalogue. See Sources and Acknowledgments, p. 205.

published in 1977 as part of the celebrations connected with the opening of the Pompidou Centre.

By 1914 Roché was in his *Jules and Jim* period, playing Jim to Franz Hessel's Jules, both devotees of Catherine.* Truffaut's film indelibly established the sounds and sights of the *Jules and Jim* era, which lasted from the outbreak of war to the late 1920s. Jeanne Moreau as Catherine in a boy's sweater and cap racing across a railway bridge, looking like Chaplin in *The Kid*, Jim and Jules doing French boxing, and the hiss of acid in a porcelain basin, kept by Catherine for 'lying eyes', became part of the currency of the 1960s. The film has charming gags, like the vignette of the anarchist who daubs on a wall *l'anarch* . . . without the *é* because he does not have enough paint.

Catherine was based upon Helen Grund, wife of Franz Hessel and a central troubling figure in Roché's life. She was a Berliner of twenty-six when she met Roché and Hessel in Paris in the autumn of 1912. She was from a Protestant banking family, a member of the class which provided Germany with pillars of society: brilliant architects, great administrators. They had connections with France. Her grandfather was honoured with the Légion d'honneur for services to France as an engineer. Helen, like Violet, wanted to be a painter. Her first lover, Mosson, established her at the Grande Chaumière. It was Franz she met first, at the Café du Dôme, and he soon fell in love with her. He told Roché that here for once there was a woman they could not share. Roché agreed, though he loved being with Helen. Unlike Franz he had many women friends, whom he took to Alésia, living himself some of the week at his mother's flat, Arago. Mme Roché never interfered, giving him meals on a tray when he wanted; they conferred briefly once a day when Pierre was staying. The temperamental refreshment he found in Mme Roché is described in both *Jules and Jim* and in *Two English*

---

* She is 'Kathe' in the novel, 'Catherine' in the film and 'Kate' in the English translation of its script. I am using Catherine for all occasions, partly because we know that Roché favoured this name because of its associations with Emily Brontë. (He told Q.D. Leavis this after she wrote him an enthusiastic letter about *Jules et Jim*, in relation to an essay she wrote comparing the Catherine of *Wuthering Heights* with Roché's.)

Girls and the Continent. He was grateful that she taught him as a child never to argue, so there was no 'whining or lamenting' to get his own way such as his school friends talked about, and 'after his adolescence, his mother had no further influence over him, except possibly to push him in the opposite direction as she always proceeded by fixed principles, and Jim was an experimentalist.'

Throughout the *Jules and Jim* period Roché was sustained by the regular devotion of Germaine Bonnard, with whom he lived a life of visiting, out of range of his mother and sequential girl-friends. Germaine appears as Gilberte in *Jules and Jim*, which gives a gentle account of the nature of their relationship. She knew how Roché lived and knew about his theories of love. They had what Roché wrote of Gilberte, 'a tacit alliance against passion', loving each other tactfully in secret, to the exclusion of their friends, meeting for one whole day a week in a room they rented, with a one-week annual holiday in the country. They did consider marrying, even consulting a doctor who advised that their offspring might not be strong. Viève promised not to stand in the way of Roché if he wanted to marry and have children. In *Jules and Jim* Gilberte/Germaine sends Jim a photograph of herself as a girl at the orphan school to which she was sent aged five after her mother's death. 'In this photo Gilberte, surrounded by her companions, looked so straightforward, trusting and helpless that Jim, without realising it, had adopted this little girl, for ever.' Roché as Jim wondered if Gilberte had other lovers, 'but as time went on it seemed more and more probable that she did not.'

In June 1913 Franz and Helen married in Berlin, not to renounce the life of free spirits, but to commit themselves fully to its onerous freedoms, agonising sincerities and brutal renunciations. They returned to Paris but, almost immediately, because of the outbreak of war, they had to go back to Germany where Franz joined the army. He wrote a study of the pre-war Parisian days called *Story of a Parisian* (*Pariser Romanze*). In *Jules and Jim* the firm friends fear that after August 1914 they might inadvertently train their rifles on each other, not a danger in reality because Roché was lucky enough to be a noncombatant – though war brought a sudden battery on his door and arrest on suspicion of espionage. He had many German contacts, including Franz. Someone outside Paris had informed on him, perhaps a jealous husband. The authorities did not find enough evidence, so he was soon at liberty and Roché wrote about the experience in a series of articles for *Le Temps*, publishing them privately in 1916 as *Two Weeks in Prison during the Battle of the Marne (Deux Semaines à la Conciergerie pendant la Bataille de la Marne)*, an early example of his penchant for binary book titles. It was characteristic of Roché to turn the experience of a moment to good effect. He proceeded to have a 'good war', exempted from conscription because of his defective knees and given an administrative post. As a correspondent for *Le Temps* he accompanied members of the American Industrial Commission on a tour of France to study the operation of industry in war time. In 1916 he was seconded to the Commission in Washington to translate its report, a task which was expected to take a few months, but in the event this and other government-related jobs kept him in New York for three years, with one period of four months in Paris. He took other work in the business world during this period, and went on writing for *Le Temps* and *The New York Times*.

In New York Roché met John Quinn, a well-off lawyer who purchased new art, painting and sculpture, and was the ideal patron to many writers. In the autumn of 1916 Roché became an aide to Quinn in his aesthetic adventures. He had always bought and sold art, loving rapid purchase, and by sales making a small income to finance his travels. From John Quinn he learned what professional dealing was like and made a distinct but discreet contribution to American culture by his acquisition for Quinn of some of the great works of the Modernist movement. Quinn had a profound impact on him: his enthusiasm, his sombreness, his air of unfulfilled romance. One female admirer wrote to Quinn from Naples to say she was watching Vesuvius and 'we are both smouldering'. Quinn was an Irish-American from Ohio, in the employ of the Governor whom he followed to the Treasury in

Washington to train there in law. He studied in Harvard under William James and George Santayana but left after a year to set up as an insurance lawyer in New York, with an interest in defending freedom in the arts. In 1911 he represented the Irish Players whose production of J. M. Synge's *The Playboy of the Western World* had been closed by the authorities. At first he collected paintings and artefacts almost indiscriminately, simply buying what he liked and driven by his powerful preferences: he loathed, for instance, Germany and its art. (When Roché suggested he buy a Paul Klee, Quinn queried whether the painter had risen 'above the grease and slime of Germany'.) In 1913 he was largely responsible for the Armory Show in New York which at a stroke introduced to America the Modernist movement in art. By then Quinn was refining and focusing his collection and, by the time he met Roché, he was only interested in what he called 'works of museum standard' or 'star pieces', almost entirely French. Quinn was politically active in the promotion of his concern for the American acquisition of treasures and potential treasures of Modernism: he fought for the recognition of a definition of 'art work' that would enable the waiving of import levies. He spent long hours dealing with the House of Representatives Sub-Committee of the Ways and Means Committee. Despite his wealth, social prestige bored him, as did any form of ostentation: he kept his paintings in rough order in an unpretentious apartment. He was as active in his assistance for writers as he was for visual artists. He famously appears in photographs with the so-called 'Three Musketeers' of literary modernism: Ford Madox Ford, James Joyce and Ezra Pound, the inspiring D' Artagnan. He encouraged authors like Joseph Conrad and T. S. Eliot with correspondence, advice and cheques. *The Waste Land* manuscript, which eventually become the property of the New York Public Library, had been purchased by Quinn to buy time for the poet. As a working lawyer he could only visit France occasionally and because of this Roché became indispensable as his scout. 'I have the impression of acting like a dog trying to raise some big birds in front of you, and you shoot them or not as it pleases you.' Quinn's detractors said he only bought from photographs, and it is true that he did use these (often commissioned from Roché's friend Man Ray, the great Modernist photographer, in Paris) but in fact Quinn never bought items unless he had actually seen other examples of the artists' works. Roché respected Quinn – he was always *Mr* Quinn in his journals – but seems also to have loved him. He wrote in a memorial essay that he had, like all 'superior spirits'

> qualities that were profound, serious, solid. Sometimes there was something seductively child-like about him, and he would laugh like a child. And then suddenly his face would recover its serenity, which was nevertheless always a bit troubled. I loved the look of him, very gentleman-like; his slimness, his distinction, his silences, his eye of an observer, even of a scrutiniser, which saw and penetrated things.

He was also fun. Ford Madox Ford remarked that, when Quinn got to France, the doors of palaces, banks and offices would fly open as if propelled by gunpowder at the approach of the piratical (Roche's word) American collector. When he was off-duty from legal practice in New York City, Quinn had Roché guide him to everything he liked best. In Paris he could argue with writers, set off on hilarious expeditions, have long frivolous lunches, so different from lawyer-lunches, and play much golf. The experience of scouting for Quinn helped Roché become a semi-professional art-dealer, developing contacts and skills which sustained him materially for the rest of his life.

Quinn depended on Roché's descriptive telegrams about paintings he had a mind to buy. The telegrams demonstrate why Roché was so useful to Quinn, but they also show the generous enthusiasm that was an integral part of Roché's nature. In 1924, not long before Quinn's death, Roché helped him make the purchase of a lifetime, Rousseau's famous *Sleeping Gipsy*: a woman in a glittery striped skirt, half lying against an azure sky, watched over by a lion, perhaps a dream animal, though the whole picture looks like a dream. In the first dispatch we see vividly 'the man who loved' with his capacity for being thrilled. Picasso had telephoned Roché in Paris to say the painting was on the market, but he had to hurry. Roché saw it, was entranced and telegrammed Quinn. (He always employed English for these communications.)

> I have seen yesterday a Rousseau which has quite upset me, it beats even the *Charmeuse* [*The Snake Charmer*] Kahnweiler has just received it. Picasso saw it there and told me to go at once, thinking of you
>> I went. It is still in his cellar, almost nobody has seen it yet. I have dreamt of it all the night.
>> It is one of the most *absolute* paintings I ever saw.
>> To me it puts in the shadow the Daumier I have sent you a photo of and the Signacs' Cézanne.
>> It has not been photo'ed yet – it is going to be.
>> I have strongly impressed Kahnweiler that you must have the first photo, that he ought to have your opinion before he exhibits the picture to the public. I do not describe it fully to you: the photo will do it.
>> There is the desert, a distant range of mountains, the night sky, a mighty strange stately lion against it; he quietly smells a big sleeping woman, lying in the foreground, she is dreaming of love, her face is *inouï*, the lion is probably going to eat her, but perhaps he will walk away.
>> I have never been more thrilled by a painting in my life.
>> The colours are equal to the composition. That is they beat for me any other of Rousseau. They are poetic, strange, simple. Perfect state of conservation.

Roché cabled New York again twenty-four hours later, again comparing the painting to Cézanne's *Snake Charmer*. 'It beats anything I know of Rousseau in sweet ghostly splendour. It has a dark soul, like the *Charmer*: it happens at moonlight.' Quinn wrote back that he had never been so impressed by 'any other work of art, it really bowled me over and prompted me to buy.'

The mystery in *The Sleeping Gipsy* delighted Roché, but in art he also valued a frank closeness of realism. Shortly before the

Rousseau purchase, he recommended a Cézanne to Quinn, the famous painting of his father, at that time inexpensive compared to the Rousseau, but not to be missed, wrote Roché, because it was 'exquisitely truthful'.

> Very cheap if compared with other Cézannes on the market – because it is rough, simple, direct, crude, almost comical in the way the old man holds his newspaper, a little 'mad' – but for me *gigantic* and genial.

Roughness, simplicity, directness, 'crudeness': the qualities are to be found in Roché's own prose and are qualities which later were to attract the young François Truffaut.

Roché made a more intimate friend in New York. He met Marcel Duchamp whose iconoclastic and 'ridiculous' art stripped down the material world and the world of concept. Duchamp was uninterested in dignity or sentiment, but certainly aware of publicity and occasion, illustrated in the varying versions of *Nude Descending a Staircase* around 1912. Duchamp carried into painting, constructions and writing, the anarchic, demure wit which Roché had loved in Jules Laforgue. Roché was involved in the practical joke played by Duchamp upon the art world in 1917. An exhibition of works of art was mounted in New York, the 'Independents', said to be the largest exhibition (1,200 contributors and 2,125 works) ever seen in the United States. Duchamp paid the required six-dollar entry fee and, after consultation and shopping with friends, submitted *Fountain*, an upended porcelain urinal with 'R. Mutt 1917' painted in black on the rim. The purpose of the exhibition was to show 'independently' what the artists rather than the critics and selectors considered to be art, all works to be displayed democratically in alphabetical order of artist, so Duchamp was entitled to have his work shown. It was voted out by the directorate, becoming as a result the best-known, but invisible (it was lost), object in the show. Almost immediately Duchamp and Roché started a little magazine called *The Blind Man* which published a credo defending the legitimacy of Richard Mutt's contribution. 'Whether Mr. Mutt with his own hands made the fountain or not has no importance. He CHOSE it. He took an ordinary article of life, placed it so that its useful significance disappeared under the new title and point of view creating a new thought for that object.' (The aesthetic argument would have been stronger had the object not been a rather beautiful piece of porcelain work – or so one presumes from the poetically lit photograph of it by Alfred Stieglitz.)

Roché admired the art that Duchamp made out of his own life, a life pared down to a condition of plainness, something to which he aspired himself, and physically he looked a little like Duchamp.

Financially, Duchamp got by on some sales, but mainly by giving two-dollar French lessons and winning chess competitions. His endearing detachment made him socially successful: Roché called him 'Totor', short for Victor, because of his success with women. Duchamp became, after Franz Hessel, the successor to Roché's original friend, Jo Jouanin, with whom he had shared girls. In his unfinished novel about Duchamp the words of Victor define the free-spirit credo of Roché and Duchamp.

> You must take either liberty or risk. Or the so-called straight path, also a risk, and children. Love without restraint becomes empty and black. Too many loves coarsen like too many whiskies. To remain yourself while loving. Not to take up residence in someone else. One mustn't eat the other or want to be eaten – it's indigestible. I refuse all the time. I refuse you. Who says I haven't wanted you.

Roché was also a refuser, seemingly greedy for experience, but in actuality cautious of indulgence, even 'continent', determined to take little: to leave a lover sooner in the afternoon than later. His sense of time was always careful to the minute – having gone, what can a lover do but visit another one? – honing an ambition to use time with austerity and searching commitment in the presence of loved ones, like Jim in *Jules and Jim*.

Lucie both admired and feared his freedom.

'As soon as Jim wants to do anything,' said Jules, 'and to the extent that he doesn't think it will hurt anybody else (he could be wrong there, though), he does it, for the pleasure and because he wants to learn something from the experience. He hopes that one day he'll achieve wisdom.'

'Surely that may take a long time?'

'We can't tell,' said Jules. 'Neither can he. After all, he might have a revelation.'

'Really!' said Lucie, one day. 'You seem to think that Jim's chaste.'

'But of course he is,' said Jules. 'All really passionate men are. He's chaster than I am, and most other men. I've known him to go without a woman for months, without even looking for one. He's not the sort that runs after someone passing in the street . . . You're a unity, and so's Jim. I'm faint with love for one thing after another in you – your feet, your hands, your lips. Direct personalities always see the other person as a whole. Some people would say Jim was always making women fall for him, but it's he who does the falling and they who make him do it. You and Gertrude and Odile, you all chose him before he chose you.'

'Or perhaps it was at the same time,' said Lucie.

His journal shows that Roché was indeed capable of following a girl who passed him in the street and at her door gravely ask for permission to begin a correspondence, but in this passage from *Jules and Jim* he is, by means of Jules as mouthpiece, describing how he saw himself, the self he wanted to be, not the pursuer, but 'the one who is chosen', the man who can therefore be free with the woman who chooses him, the woman who is unpersuaded by him. This was the mental trick or device which, of course, yields a return of intimacies to the reserved man (or woman). Such a person may be called a Casanova, but if so, then it is a mark of the Casanova not to be a seducer, but one who is available. This conversation between Jules and Lucie describes what Truffaut later called Roché's 'aesthetic morality', possessed also by Duchamp whose own life, Roché thought, was more of an art-work than his exhibitable artefacts. Duchamp's best art was, he said, 'the way he used his time'. Jokes and poker-faced joyousness characterised Roché's friendship with Duchamp: 'larking', in fact, nicely shown in a snapshot of Roché taken, probably by Franz Hessel, in some seaside sand hills just after the war.

Roché was lucky with his war, unlike his fictional self, Jim. But on the other side, the war was hard for Franz and Helen. Ulrich, their first child, was born in July 1914, then Stéphane in 1917. Ulrich had slight brain damage so Stéphane played the part of both elder and younger brother to Ulrich. The boys hardly saw their father in the infant years. Helen was remembered by Stéphane as their Aphrodite. After the war Helen insisted on going back to the land to do agricultural work and the placid Franz went along with the plan, as with all Helen's wishes, though city life suited him best as a writer, translator and journalist. He was mentally withdrawn after the war, exhausted by it and indeed by Helen. All his loving stoicism was required to earn a living by his pen with her in rural Bavaria.

At the end of 1919 Roché returned from America and made his way to a reunion with the Hessels, enthralled to see Franz whom he kissed on the lips when they met. He found a strained family, with Franz and Helen affectionate but chaste. Then in August 1920 Roché and the four of them went for a summer holiday near Hohenschäftlarn in Bavaria. Helen walked out one night with Roché across the fields for three hours. The physical relationship of Franz and Helen had faded: he was 'le soldat qui dort' and she 'helped him to be happy'. Roché had always thought she was irresistible, inexhaustible and unpredictable, the free spirit. (He likened her to Margaret, surprisingly, because it was Violet who was the bohemian, attic-studio-dwelling sister.) He wrote in his journal that until now he had waited for Helen, honouring the no-sharing-this-time pledge to Franz with 'a respectful patience' – it had felt like the suspension of his relationship with Margaret – but soon after their nocturnal walk Roché and Helen became lovers. Franz was gently considerate to them, relieved, at last, to find Helen happy. He would tactfully remind them to separate before the boys came in when he brought their breakfast coffee in bed. The Hessels moved to Munich and then Berlin, where Franz became increasingly known as a man-of-letters, combining, said his son Stéphane in his autobiography, the penetration or *éclairage* of Brecht with the melancholy of Walter Benjamin (with whom Franz planned to make a translation of Proust). Franz tried to make a condition with Helen that she should not become pregnant. Over this issue the seemingly collaborative though unorthodox family soon divided. Roché and Helen wanted a child (particularly a son), though their relationship was erratic, a daily duel of love (Roché called it: 'tender, deep, with crises of distrust, jealousy, hatred, with the partial madness, the partial genius of love. Is this better or worse for conceiving a son?') He returned periodically to France, to infidelities detected by a savagely judicious Helen. Helen demanded a divorce from Franz and got it, but she naturally wanted Roché to give up his Parisian life and the long-standing companionship of Viève.

Roché was also emerging as an author. He had written much journalism, but in 1921 published the first book close to his intimate life and personal philosophy. *Don Juan* was written under the pseudonym of 'Jean Roc', to spare the feelings of Mme Clara Roché. Since 1907 he had been working on a set of stories and a poem about the adventures of an amorist. As Ashton and Lake pointed out in *Henri Pierre: An Introduction*, Roché gives the loves of Don Juan a 'cautious religious resonance'. A God is imagined as One who does with the world what 'we do with the women he has given us'. The lover constructs or rehabilitates. This concept revives Roché's early idea of 'The Work', conceived in the trio years earlier in London, at the time when his erotic education was coinciding with realisations about exploitative capitalism.

Although he had fared better in the war than Franz and Helen, Roché had his own losses in the post-war decade.

John Quinn died in 1924 of cirrhosis (though he rarely drank alcohol) at the age of fifty-five. Roché was called immediately to New York by his friends where he had to arrange for the disposition of Quinn's collection of works of art, which was in a chaotic state. He lived in Quinn's apartment for two weeks, obliged to make decisions about the disposal of his trove of

Modernist masterpieces, which he discreetly succeeded in doing. Roché then travelled around America with the director of the Théâtre National de l'Odéon and his theatre company after the loss of his father figure, Quinn.

In 1925 he settled in France again. Helen had insisted on moving to Paris to be near him, though Germans were still hated in France. Franz could find plenty of translation work in Paris. In many respects it was delightful for them to replace the dank Berlin of Rilke with the playfulness of Paris, the world in which Satie and Apollinaire were now established. Helen was able to live by her pen: she had a fashion column in the *Frankfurter Zeitung* which was regularly posted off. She and Franz were at the heart of the art world. Alexander Calder's delicate hanging steel petals were first called 'mobiles' in the playroom of their children, Ulrich and Stéphane. Roché was to hand, a pleasing 'uncle', the elegant beanstalk who taught the boys ducks-and-drakes and loaned Stéphane his Parker pen. Franz read them Homer, Grimm and Wilhelm Busch in his precise articulation, with a delight in word-play. The long conversation between friends seemed to have renewed itself, but not for long. A new trio was fashioned.

Roché had sometimes thought about Violet and Margaret, as his post-war journals show, but there was no contact with them. Then, on a visit to London in 1927, he learned that Margaret had died the previous year. He had a letter from Violet.

She died of cancer on March 17th, 1926. She was marvellously brave, meaning with a strong will to live. Others would have given in long before. We did not know she had cancer till the last few weeks. She had been seriously ill from pneumonia, then jaundice twice in the last two years, but had pulled through wonderfully with her strong will. It is even now sometimes difficult to realise that she is no longer visible on this earth. It is the first death of anyone very close to me that I have known. But in November Mother died and a fortnight ago Stephen's wife and these gaps have left life ever different.

Mother was eighty-three and her time had come doubtless, but strangely or not I miss her very, very greatly. She had been so well till a few months before but the shock of Margaret's death was too much. She died in an asylum.

Young Margaret survived, now aged twelve. Roché visualised her as the girl in the photograph of her mother which Violet had shown him in Paris in 1899.

Paris was sweeter for Franz and Helen than Berlin, but their lives were soon under threat. Helen wanted Roché, but he would not give up Viève, who now lived in an apartment which he owned in the Rue Froidevaux, and in fact in December 1927 he and Viève married suddenly and as secretly as they had linked their lives for over twenty years. Helen remarried Franz. The bare facts suggest the beginning of a new stability, but this was far from the case. Two other events catalysed the confusion and pain which followed. First, even though he had just married, Roché met another woman, Denise Renard, who told him she was desperate to have a child. Second, in March 1929, Mme Clara Coquet Roché died at the age of eighty, living as ever in the apartment in Rue d'Arago, with occasional but few friendly visitors and going to the cinema by herself almost to the end. Her death haunted Roché. He had a recurring dream in which she and John Quinn appeared to him. On the night after her death Roché made love with Denise Renard for the first time. He was now affronting both Viève and Helen and failing in the control that he had tried to exercise as his own type of Casanova. He was physically less capable of running the life he had planned years ago after his readings of Nietzsche and Schopenhauer, but he was closing into stability with Denise: she was often ill, and only recovered with difficulty from an operation for breast cancer, but in September 1930 she was indeed pregnant and her son was born on 11 May 1931. Roché had hoped to call his son 'Pierre-Denis', a curious linkage of Denise and Pierre (reminiscent of Margaret's daughter being given her name), but he became Jean-Claude. Viève found the situation intolerable. She had to bear Pierre's infidelity in a new form, and tolerate now the attentions of Helen of whom she was not only jealous, but from whom she received sanctimonious and intellectualised advice by letter. In 1933 she broke with Roché and thenceforth would only communicate by letter, and she adamantly refused a divorce: 'Your name is mine.' So Denise was only able to take the name of Roché years later, when she married him six weeks after the death of Viève in April 1948.

Viève rebelled and so did Helen. She was not told about the birth of Jean-Claude and only discovered this unbearable fact in July 1933. She went to Rue d'Arago and drew a gun on Roché. He retained some of his boxer's nimbleness and managed to survive. She and Franz returned to Germany. Helen swore she was leaving Roché for ever and she kept her promise. For the sake of Franz, Roché never attempted to see her again. Denise had now the central place for him. The place of Margaret or Helen or Germaine, or Clara Coquet?

Now in the 1930s, after the burning of the Reichstag in Berlin and the rise of Nazism, Roché was a middle-aged man in his fifties who had lost some of his dearest ones to death (Quinn, Margaret and his mother). In Violet and Margaret he had invented sisters, and invented brothers in Franz and Duchamp. Quinn had been a kind of father, though only ten years his senior. He had not seen Margaret since 1909, and she was now gone. He had not seen Violet for even longer, since 1907, and had not tried: he knew her husband was a jealous man. Franz and Helen Hessel had remarried and departed for Germany – but in 1936 Helen divorced Franz again because of the anti-semitism in Germany, even though Franz was only part Jewish. He moved to France in 1938 and another war began. At home Franz was regarded as a Jew and in France he was known to be a German, and so was lodged in a series of internment camps in which his health gave way. He was released during the war, but he died in January 1941.

Roché did not learn of the death of Franz until over a year later (as he did not learn of Margaret's). He was deeply shaken:

here was another loss in another land. He had always thought that he would eventually see Franz again.

> How we counted on having the leisure to continue one day our eternal conversations. We didn't write to each other, see each other, out of fear of and pity of Helen – and we truly thought that, with her love for risk-taking and for the absolute, God would call her before us. This death for me is such a deep sorrow, and not to have been able to help him. Helen's violence, and her revolver, were always between us.

During the war Roché was in the south of France, having moved into the unoccupied zone, like many of those in the art world. He was teaching at the École de Beauvallon, living with Denise, and of course never seeing Viève. In 1942 he began a different kind of writing, increasingly preoccupied with his own past history, and especially with Franz. He wanted something to survive of the friendship and the conversations. He had plenty of material which enshrined his years before the 1914–1918 war – letters from Franz, his own journals, and many letters and a journal by Helen, which she called 'Roché-Grund'. But it was all far away to the north, in occupied Paris, divided between Rue d'Alésia and Rue d'Arago, so he had to rely on his memory. He thought of writing a film about Franz, hopefully to be made by Jean Renoir, called *The Solo Man* (*L'Homme Unique*) for which by early 1943 he had finished an outline; but memories of Helen overwhelmed him and he stopped. He was struggling to write something, 'so that others will benefit from it', as Margaret had said about herself and Pierre forty years earlier. In the summer of 1943 he felt he had a solution. 'I am definitely writing *Jules and Jim* – where Franz plays the leading role.'

Roché worked very fast on *Jules and Jim*, completing his first draft in forty days. 'It flows readily, like blood from a good cut.' There was then much re-writing for about three years. In 1946 the finished manuscript was sent to the publisher Gaston Gallimard, whom Roché had known in his New York days when Gallimard was the administrator of a visiting French theatre group. There were many delays, but eventually *Jules and Jim* appeared in March 1953. It won the Claire Belon Prize. Violet Court had died three years before and (again) Roché was unaware that a loved one had gone.

Those who know Truffaut's *Jules and Jim* usually find the novel familiar or 'cinematic' with its use of brief chapters and sudden diversions, but are sometimes surprised that the story is not so simply one of Jules, Jim and Catherine supplemented by walk-on parts. The real events of the lives are shown fairly closely, though to the exclusion of the activities of both Roché and Hessel as intellectuals. Nearly a third of the original novel is about the friends and the life of all kinds of free spirits, and before the arrival of Catherine on the scene in Part III, there is an ominous, dream-like prelude. The friends are staying in the country and take a winter walk during which they play a sinister game. Seeing crows wheeling overhead, Jim tells Jules to wrap himself in his brown cape, then stumble, fall and get up every twenty metres, like an injured animal. He does so and quickly the birds descend for carrion 'like an inverted waterspout'. Jim is frightened they will attack Jules's eyes in the vortex, so he fires a shot to dispel them, at first without success. Jules, who does not see the danger, is delighted by the trick, but 'Jim was stirred, as if by some symbol which was beyond his comprehension.' It is the exciting Catherine who descends and she attacks at the end of the novel, but attacks Jim. Jim is seen in Paris with three women, 'Gilberte [Germaine] came to see him in the morning, Catherine [Helen] after lunch and Michèle [Denise] in the evening.' Jim resolves to tell Catherine he wants to have a child with Michèle (in reality, as we have seen, the revelation comes after the child is born) and Catherine at first appears sympathetic and deeply moved. She sweetly congratulates Jim on the decision, but her face changes: 'She was becoming a Gorgon.' (Elsewhere in the novel she alluded to as Penthesilea, Queen of the Amazons.) She demands Jim's revolver and manages to lock them both in his

apartment, but he fights her off. However, soon after she tricks
Jim into her car and drives it on to a bridge with an unfinished
parapet. 'Watch us carefully, Jules!' she cries as they disappear
to their deaths. Truffaut is shockingly faithful to this part of
the novel.

On the publication of *Jules and Jim* in 1953 Roché was
seventy-four years old, settled with Denise and his son was
grown up. He wanted to write more. He could now write
differently about the past because he had his papers with
him. For years he had thought about making something out
of his collection of diaries and letters relating to his youth,
including those of Violet and Margaret. In April he was
working on this new book. He experimented with several
titles:

Deux Anglaises
Deux Anglaises et le Continent
Deux Soeurs
Anne and Muriel
Deux Soeurs Anglaises
Une Puritaine
Le Grand Nord

On 14 June 1955 he tried to encapsulate his concept in this
vignette:

A Gentle Story of Three Friends
There were once three incomparable friends, Muriel, Anne
and Claude. Muriel had red hair and Anne had brown. They
were sisters and English. All three were orphaned of their
fathers. They played together at first like children on a
beach.

Roché's preparation for writing included brief character-
sketches of Claude, Anne and Muriel, written up in three
columns.

ANNE	MURIEL	CLAUDE
Independent. Diana-type. Comrade. Friend. Curious: a bit sensual. No question of children. But sculpture. Wants Claude to make her a woman. Idealist for her sculpture. No pride of [sic] anger	Divided – alternate type: 'prophet'. Altruism. Pious. Redhead (father). Pride, anger. *Born Writer*. Realist, mystical. Intelligence. *Napoleonism*. Actress. Given to multiple domains.	A modest master. But: learns, writes. Quick angers and indignation. Ambitious for his work

His papers allowed Roché to write a documentary novel which foregrounded his sources, the letters and journal-extracts, rather than one written in the pithy but conventional style of *Jules and Jim*. The finished product looks as if real materials are reproduced, but nearly every piece included in the mosaic was carefully rewritten and interspersed with inventions. When short of material, Roché made it up to look like the real thing. For example, the novel begins with a short chapter consisting of three journal entries headed 'Easter, 1899', '15 May 1899', and '25 June 1899'. No diary survives with these entries in it and where diaries do survive the material in them sometimes contradicts what appears to be authentic history in the novel. Because Margaret's Paris diary exists her account of what happened can be checked against the novel, and when it is, it is clear that Roché's policy was to stress how little Muriel assimilated herself to Paris and how fully Anne did so. (The process is taken even further in Truffaut's film of the novel in which Muriel is given no early experience of Paris at all and is presented as the purely stay-at-home sister.) There are changes in chronology: Henri Pierre Roché did meet the waif-like woman whom the girls' dubbed 'Hope' (after Watts's painting), but at a different time from the one given in the novel. Once he retrieved his papers from Paris, Roché transformed them and fictionalised them.

Two English Girls and the Continent was finished in 1955 and published in April 1956. Shortly before the novel came out Roché wrote several pieces to help the publisher with publicity. Gaston Gallimard thought that it would be interesting to play up the fact that Roché began to write novels so late in life (which was indeed to capture the attention of Truffaut). So Roché wrote a short essay probably destined to be a blurb for the back cover, but it was too long. It epitomises the novel.

Eighty Years Old!

My eightieth year is approaching. Decrepitude? Perhaps, but I hardly notice it. What a panorama! What sweet breaths of wind at this summit. One has one's whole life before one, like a nearly perfect sphere.

One of the games I play every evening before going to sleep.

In parallel, I focus on a period of my life and I let it gently unroll, each evening, like a film in episodes.

Among my memories there is a great ball, a mysterious ball. At the end of my adolescence, full of lights, and struggles, joys, agonies, contrarieties, full of regret and hidden treasures, too. For three years I have been unravelling this ball, and putting it together again, like a puzzle.

The facts: two English sisters, between eighteen and twenty, Muriel and Anne, and myself, Claude, French, eighteen years old [actually nineteen], all three of us full of ideas that were advanced for 1899, making up a trio of friends, studying, playing, travelling together without flirtation. Two years flow by.

We innocently scandalise their little English town and the mother of the two sisters requests me to cease my visits. I cannot stay away, especially from Muriel, whom I ask to marry me.

A cold Puritan, she firmly says 'No', but she offers to continue to be my sister. I try this. Anne helps us. Three months later our mothers intervene, on account of 'our health'. We accept that we should separate for one year. I am sure that Muriel will never love me, and I commit myself to study and celibacy, which choice moves Muriel towards a 'Yes'.

After a great deal of travelling hither and thither, Anne and I take up with each other again. One beautiful day in Paris she lets me cover her young breast in her hand. Later, by a Swiss lake, although she is still half a boy, she lets me take her. She has to go away and live some of this time at home in England. Muriel, recovered, comes to see me for an hour when crossing Paris. To our astonishment she gives me one kiss, without speaking. When she has gone home she keeps a journal about love which she will not let me see.

At a distance I love both of them. Muriel tells Anne that she is in love with me, and Anne says that she and I have been lovers. After a year Muriel returns to give herself and to take me. Anne writes from the Caucasus, to say that she will marry a friend of a Russian lover she once had in Paris. Muriel comes and gives herself. We are together for three short days. We think of marrying. But race, our ways of life, religions, studies – and the Channel – hold us back, and become obstacles. We love each other, but, in spite of ourselves, we pull back. (In England they drive on the left, in France on the right.) Four years later Muriel marries an 'ordinary' Englishman.

I have re-lived my youth in unravelling these threads, I am also making a confession. Perhaps it will interest people who are young today.

Roché also wrote a straightforward, factually dense blurb for the novel which was eventually used by the publisher. It captures some of the romantic quality of the story by its use of a traditional metaphor: 'The first arrow strikes Muriel. The second arrow strikes Anne.'

There was another piece of publicity, devised by the publisher's office, which was emphatically not used. French books often have a *bande*, a paper strip with a slogan on it, folded round them. In this case an editor or publicist decided it should read: *LOVE BEGINS AT CALAIS*. The normally benign Roché angrily contacted Gallimard's office. This cliché had a francophiliac smugness which was absolutely contrary to the spirit of *Two English Girls and the Continent*. Contrite, the publisher changed his *bande* to a sentence of Roché's own invention: *WHAT, THEN, IS LOVE?*

Roché's journey had been long. We were introduced to Roché in the drawing-room of his parental home, the apartment of Mme Clara Roché, seen here photographed in about 1907.

After the war he kept the apartment and used it to store some of the items in his art collection, as we see him here, a half-century of changed taste later.

But by the time Roché made a new friend after *Jules and Jim*, he and Denise had settled outside Paris.

It is the late 1950s and Paris is recovering from occupation and liberation. It has found existentialism and in the cinema the *auteur*. Now François Truffaut enters the story of Henri Pierre Roché and the two English girls.

Chapter Five

françois truffaut enters

The trio had dissolved, the individuals separated and, over forty years later, a new person entered the story of Pierre, Violet and Margaret. In 1956 the young François Truffaut met the old Henri Pierre Roché, became his friend, and in due course filmed both his novels, awarding him, at least for *Jules and Jim* (1962), world-wide popularity. His version of *Two English Girls and the Continent*, made much later in 1971, was not successful at the time, but in recent years it has acquired increasing respect and been recognised as a work intimately close to its director, especially since the publication in 1996 of the biography of Truffaut by Antoine de Baecque and Serge Toubiana. In this chapter we are going to see how and why Truffaut joined the world of Roché and the English girls, first showing how he met Roché, then briefly tracing Truffaut's career through the 1960s up to the point at which he made *The Two English Girls and the Continent*, and finally showing what happened to Roché's novel and the English girls at his hands. Truffaut's film had the same title as the novel, but here it is called *Anne and Muriel* so as not to become confused with the novel.

In the autumn of 1955 François Truffaut was browsing in the trays of a second-hand book shop in Paris called Libraire Stock, in the Place Palais Royale. He was twenty-three years old, had suffered an abortive period in the army from which he deserted and now lived a hand-to-mouth journalistic life, saturated by the cinema. His routine was a film every day and often an article or listings piece every two days. He had achieved his ambition to write for the *nouvelle vague* journal *Cahiers du Cinéma*, founded two years earlier. As a film-maker Truffaut had so far only accomplished *A Visit*, a ten-minute production made with friends in five days. His first feature film, *The 400 Blows*, which made his name, was a few years away.

In the Stock book trays he was attracted by the sight of *Jules and Jim*, published two years earlier, noticing first the double J on the cover, and then was intrigued to learn from the publisher's note that this was a first novel by a man of seventy-four. In this period Truffaut was interested in old masters of literature and cinema, the 'great tutelary figures', as he called them. When he was nineteen Truffaut had written to Jean Genet who gave him a friendly reception, and he became the adoptive son of the critic André Bazin. He wrote to a friend in this period that in three months Genet and Bazin had done more for him than his parents had managed in fifteen years. As a critic he had made a point of approaching the master film directors (Buñuel, Jean Renoir, Abel Gance, Nicholas Ray), introducing himself by letter and asking if he could listen to them talk, or shadow them on film. He had a particularly successful taped interview with Max Ophuls in 1953 which was published in *Cahiers du Cinéma*.

Truffaut bought the novel *Jules and Jim* and was entranced, particularly because he noticed that the subject, the triangular relationship between two men and a woman, was mirrored in a low-budget Hollywood film of that season which he much admired, *The Naked Dawn* (also known as *Bandit*), directed by Edgar Ulmer. He liked both this film and Roché's novel because of their neutrality in treating the three members of a trio, no single one morally preferred. Ulmer's film was, he thought, 'an intimate Western' in which the audience was not forced to take sides. He reviewed *The Naked Dawn* for the 14 March issue of *Arts-Spectacles*, making a comparison between it and *Jules and Jim*. Roché happened to read the review: he was delighted to see his work praised by one who must be a young man, a cinema enthusiast and an Americanophile. *Two English*

Girls and the Continent was about to be published and Roché arranged for a copy to be sent to the reviewer. He wrote to Truffaut on 11 April 1956.

> I was very touched by your few words about *Jules and Jim* in *Arts*, especially your phrases about the interest of the novel owing much to a sense of a fresh 'aesthetic' morality, perpetually re-thinking itself. I hope you will find this morality even more vividly present in my recent novel *Two English Girls and the Continent*. You will receive it shortly!

Roché was now living in the suburbs of Paris with his wife Denise Renard, but he still visited the city frequently. Truffaut received an invitation to come for the afternoon and a friendship began.

Truffaut would go down to Meudon to see Roché at his little house with the railway at the end of his garden. He announced that he would make a film of *Jules and Jim*. (He later decided to do *Two English Girls and the Continent* as well, but this was more of a promise to himself than to Roché in person.) Many years before, Gertrude Stein had said Roché was a 'very earnest, very noble, devoted, very faithful and enthusiastic man.' Truffaut was similarly faithful to his artistic mentors, but he could not yet bring to fruition what he had promised. So far he had too little standing in the film industry to make the expensively set and costumed historical film that *Jules and Jim* would have to be. It may seem strange that Truffaut wanted to make a costume picture about bohemians of the *belle époque*. One could explain his desire by reference to the bohemian subject-matter (which related to his own hand-to-mouth writing and on-the-edge life in a Paris now exhilaratedly recovered from the occupation) and to the evident attractions of Roché's morality (the wise neutrality). But the power of Roché's style must not be forgotten, a style with which Truffaut believed he could do something on film. The writing style of *Jules and Jim* struck him 'like a blow', he wrote in an essay on 'Henri-Pierre Roché Revisité', used as an introduction to the first published volume of Roché's journal.

> At that time my favourite writer was Jean Cocteau for the rapidity of his seemingly dry sentences and the precision of his imagery. Roché was the *stronger*, attaining a similar poetry in prose by the use of a smaller and less arcane vocabulary, and using ultra-short sentences with everyday words. Within the texture of this style emotion was, as it were, created in the spaces between the words on Roché's page, in the sensed absences of words, the spaces for the sake of which words had been rejected. The very ellipses created meanings.

Later, when he saw Roché's manuscripts, Truffaut learned that the curt style was created by endless revision. Truffaut called it a 'rejecting' ('raturé') style. Roché's drafts were palimpsests of correction and especially of elimination.

> I saw that the studiedly simple was created by a huge percentage of words and sentences crossed out. In one page covered with a round school-boy hand, Roché would finally allow seven or eight sentences to survive, with two-thirds of them crossed with deletions. *Jules and Jim* is a novel written like a telegram, written by a poet who forces himself to forget his cultivation and to align his words and thoughts as if they were coming with the concreteness of laconic, peasant speech.

Truffaut's early films were made with a similar naiveté of style, with roughness, concreteness, variability. Truffaut tried to persuade Roché to write some film dialogue in this style, 'aerés et serrés'. He demurred, though he said he knew a little about dramatic writing, having once tried to translate Chekhov's *Uncle Vanya*. He told Truffaut to read *Mon Amant se marie* by Thora Dardsel, which he said he had translated but not published in 1905.

Truffaut's visits continued. In 1958 he excitedly announced to Roché that he was going to be able to make his first (relatively cheap) feature film, *The 400 Blows*, about a Truffaut-like boy on the edge of delinquency. He had persuaded Jeanne Moreau, already a star, to play an improvised cameo rôle, having loved her stage performance as Maggie in Tennessee Williams's *Cat on a Hot Tin Roof*. He was convinced she would be ideal for Catherine in *Jules and Jim*. Truffaut posted Roché some photographs of her and received a swift reply.

> My young friend, your good letter! Thank you so much for the photos of Jeanne Moreau. She pleases me. I'm happy she likes Kathe [Catherine]! I hope to meet her one day. Yes, come and see me when you want.

Roché wrote this on 5 April 1959 and six days later he died. The novelist's approval symbolised his affinity with Truffaut. They shared a liking for the same types of women and for the same type of life with women. Roché's pleasure at the photographs of Moreau was a blessing, an *imprimatur*.

The 400 Blows (1959) was duly made and at the age of twenty-seven Truffaut won Best Director prize at Cannes and fifteen other prizes. The president of the jury was none other than Jean Cocteau, still a favourite author of Truffaut's, who keenly promoted him. The leading player in *The 400 Blows* was Jean-Pierre Léaud who showed Antoine Doinel growing up in three-and-a-half sequels (three films and a segment in a compilation film). After *The 400 Blows*, Truffaut went on to make another hit, the anarchic *Shoot the Piano Player*, and he was now able to keep his promise to Roché. *Jules and Jim* was made, indeed with Jeanne Moreau as Catherine. Henri Serre played Jim and Oskar Werner was Jules. It was a great success of 1962 and its wit, scepticism and freedom became part of the atmosphere of the 1960s. It was one of the first French CinemaScope pictures, and, when the screen lit into a title-sequence backed by headlong dance music, audiences felt they were experiencing a fresh type of period gaiety. There had been Jean Renoir's *French Can Can* of 1955, but this new film about old Paris was excitingly all over the place: it was contemporary (CinemaScope), but, unlike

French Can Can, it was in black-and-white. Its do-what-you-like style and how-to-do-tricks sequences (how to use a cigarette to be a steam-train; how to put the names of French wines into verse) was what the era wanted. The peaceful Jules was an early hippie, the trio's open relationship beguilingly communitarian and Jeanne Moreau's guitar playing and singing of 'Love's Whirlwind' ('Le Tourbillon') had great charm. It was not readily grasped that *tourbillon* means whirlpool as well as a whirlwind, and the film's bleak conclusion (Jules stiffly following caskets containing the ashes of Catherine and Jim) was much harsher than the end of the novel and little regarded. The film became an international hit. In 1962 Pauline Kael, later doyenne of film critics in *The New Yorker*, wrote in San Francisco that the film 'carries us along without pauses for reflection. Truffaut doesn't linger; nothing is held too long, nothing is overstated or even *stated*.' She made fun of the New York critic Stanley Kauffmann who had written that Truffaut 'confused the sheer happiness of making a film with the reason for making it.' Kael retorted that Truffaut needed no reason for making a film, any more than Picasso needed reason for picking up a brush. 'He works everywhere and with anything at hand.'

Jules and Jim was translated all over the world and Henri Pierre Roché became the *Jules and Jim* man. Stéphane, the now grown-up son of Helen and Franz, was amused when people said he must be the daughter of Catherine and Jules (who in the film have the little girl, Sabine, who sings with her mother, but no son). However, Roché's other novel, *Two English Girls and the Continent*, was not carried into public acclaim in the wake of *Jules et Jim*. But Truffaut did not forget it and actually became increasingly absorbed by thoughts of his old friend. Denise Renard let him study Roché's daily journal, the *Carnets* going back to 1904, in which he could read the real story of Violet and Margaret and much else besides. Truffaut was now a prosperous film producer with his own company, Les Films de Carrosse. He employed one of his stenographers to make a typed copy of the *Carnets*, which finally ran to several hundred pages. Later Truffaut said that hardly a day passed without his browsing in the typescript – which had not been produced without difficulty: more than one typist gave up, unable to face constant exposure to Roché's daily life, not only his sexual frankness, but the unremitting intimacy of his observation. The resignation of one such typist forms a touching episode in Truffaut's 1977 film, *The Man Who Loved Women*, which is based on his felt knowledge of Roché – and is not 'about Truffaut', as has been suggested. (Truffaut makes a momentary, Hitchcock-like appearance at the beginning of the film, watching, perhaps forlornly, from the kerb-side the funeral cortège of the film's 'man who loved women'.) As for *Two English Girls and the Continent*, he still wanted to film it. He had a draft screenplay produced by Jean Gruault, friend and long-standing collaborator, though after much struggle with the novel, Gruault could only come up with a script of over 500 pages, much longer than a normal screenplay. Truffaut abandoned the project and it did not surface again until 1971, after and as a result of a crisis in Truffaut's fortunes. Meanwhile, Truffaut's golden period of the 1960s proceeded apace.

In the 1960s, in the decade after the death of Roché, Truffaut became the most successful young maker of non-English-speaking films in the world. The nearest rival was Roman Polanski. The scale of Truffaut's reputation can be judged, paradoxically, by his involvement in two unsuccessful projects in this period. In 1964 it was Truffaut who was engaged to make *Bonnie and Clyde* with Hollywood stars: Jane Fonda and Lesley Caron had been considered before Faye Dunaway became Bonnie Parker. Truffaut withdrew because he did not want to work with Warren Beatty, but the offer of this film was an index of his acceptability in Hollywood. Then in 1965 Truffaut was able to complete a project which was dear to him, a film of Ray Bradbury's novel *Fahrenheit 451* for which he had bought the rights. When it appeared in 1966 the film was unpopular and undervalued, but the fact that it was financed by Universal was a tribute to Truffaut's bankability, as was the fact that he was able to make the film without any concession to conventional ideas of science fiction. (He cast Julie Christie to play two rôles and Oskar Werner to play Montag and, when asked if the design of the film would look like Courregès' futuristic fashion, he said that he had asked his designer, the unfuturistic Tony Walton, to give the film the look of a Debbie Reynolds picture.)

In Europe of course Truffaut built up a striking body of work. He made ten films before 1970, of which three were very successful indeed (*The 400 Blows, Shoot the Piano Player, Jules and Jim*). By the end of the decade he was so confident that he could film almost anything he liked. Thus in 1969 he made a very specialised film, *The Wild Child*, in black-and-white, about Jean Itard, the eighteenth-century psychologist and *philosophe*, who experimented with the education of a feral child, a 'wolf boy' recovered from a forest in Aveyron. Truffaut played Itard himself.

During the 1960s Truffaut's personal life was chaotic, after the manner of Roché. He married Madeleine Morgenstern and the match was happy, except that he had numerous love-affairs, in one phase slipping out often from their marital apartment for cigarettes in order to spend an hour with a girl-friend. He was divorced in 1965, but with a relative lack of rancour. He had two daughters whom he saw frequently. Other love affairs followed, including a brief and intensely affectionate one with Françoise Dorléac who died (when they were no longer lovers) in a car crash on the road to Nice airport in 1967. When Truffaut made *Stolen Kisses* (1968) he wanted to marry the twenty-year-old actress Claude Jade who played the female lead, but it seems she proved too much a character of the student generation of 'May '68' for a relationship with Truffaut. He soon became seriously involved with the sister of Françoise Dorléac, Catherine Deneuve. In June 1969 they moved into an apartment in the fashionable Rue Saint-Guillaume.

Catherine Deneuve had acted for Buñuel and Polanski. She had been a fashion model, featured in Chanel advertising as the 'most beautiful woman in the world'. She was a pragmatic and cheerful person: in one of the crew photographs for *The Wild Child*, reproduced in De Baecque and Toubiana's biography of

Truffaut, she is sitting next to the director with the merriest of smiles. Catherine Deneuve was about Truffaut's age, a distinct advantage over Claude Jade, and they were delighted to have found each other. They lived with Catherine's son, Christian. It was the first time Truffaut had actually lived with a woman since his separation from his wife.

In 1969 Catherine starred for Truffaut in his *Mississippi Mermaid* with Jean-Paul Belmondo. It was for Truffaut a big picture with stars and glamorous locations. Some members of the French film intelligentsia were sarcastic about what appeared to be a pseudo-Hollywood confection. The film did not have the quirky, good-enough-for-jazz quality associated with Truffaut. Some critics asked if he had sold out like Charlie Kohler in his earlier film *Shoot the Piano Player*. Truffaut certainly had a taste for commercial success and also respectability. Jean-Luc Godard remarked that François was a businessman in the morning and a poet in the afternoon. Truffaut observed himself that, at a political demonstration in 1968 in which Jean-Paul Sartre participated, it was the Nobel prize-winner in a stained leather jacket who was taken away by the police, not the suited Truffaut. With Catherine Deneuve he had become still smarter: she persuaded him to buy suits from Lanvin rather than Cardin and shoes from Berlutti.

We see in Truffaut's 1960s a rising curve. But there was an event which was troubling at a deep level, a knowledge of which helps to show how and why Truffaut decided finally in 1971 to translate *Two English Girls and the Continent* into film. Truffaut's mother, Janine, died in August 1968, for him a moment of reassessment in, as we shall see, a literal sense, and a moment in which he was faced with responsibility for the harsh picture of the mother of Antoine Doinel in *The 400 Blows*, the story which the world understood to be autobiographical.

Truffaut was born to Janine de Montferrand in February 1932 when she was not yet twenty and had no husband but plenty of boy-friends. Janine lived at home where her pregnancy was not noticed until the third month; the infant François was ignored, by boarding him out as long as possible after the hushed-up birth. It cannot be known how often Janine visited the infant, but it is clear that the father disappeared from the scene. Twenty months after François's birth Janine became engaged to Roland Truffaut, who legally recognised the boy as an adoptive child, but the habit of distance, with François in the hands of carers, was now established and the child continued to live mostly away from his parents. Janine and Roland had a child of their own who died in infancy. The young Truffaut's health was poor: his grandmother intervened and took control of him first in Paris, and then in Brittany to which she moved at the outbreak of war. She died in 1942 so a decision had to be made about the boy who now moved in with his parents, and within a couple of years a life began which *approximated* to that shown in *The 400 Blows*. Janine and Roland were less rackety than the film parents of Antoine Doinel. Janine was a reader and theatre-goer, as well as having love-affairs, and Roland was a keen walker and climber. Janine was motherly by fits and starts. It seems that during his childhood Janine had been neglectful, hectoring and Truffaut had disliked her, but was also emotionally in awe of her. In *The 400 Blows* Antoine has an inseparable friend based on Truffaut's real friend Robert Lachenay: he told the biographers that Truffaut respected Janine, that he thought she was an admirably independent woman. In Truffaut's wedding photographs she is a strikingly attractive presence. His step-father, Roland, was a tall, joking man; in the wedding photographs he resembles Henri Serre as Jim in *Jules and Jim*, chosen because of his resemblance to Roché. The shy Truffaut had an affinity with Jules, and with the Jules-like Montag of *Fahrenheit 451*, a secret reader whose psychological refuge was *David Copperfield*. Truffaut was something of a David Copperfield as a child, and perhaps later. Unlike Jules or Montag (both played by Oskar Werner) Truffaut was wiry, small, and could be febrile and aggressive. Early in this period Truffaut doubted that Roland Truffaut was his natural father, having discovered one of Roland's old diaries in which significant events were recorded, but no entry made for his birth.

The death of Janine de Montferrand in 1968 (from cirrhosis, like John Quinn) was particularly difficult for Truffaut. He knew he had created in the public mind a sense that she was a bad mother and that he had suffered from parental neglect. People had been shocked at the cruel carelessness of the parents of Antoine Doinel in *The 400 Blows* and Antoine had become irredeemably associated with Truffaut himself. It was presumed that Truffaut suffered like Antoine and he never really denied it. If his own parents were not quite like the film parents, at any rate it seemed that their effect must have been similar. As a result Truffaut could not expect much sympathy from Janine's family at her death.

The funeral of Janine de Montferrand was therefore a trial. After the death of Françoise Dorléac Truffaut had vowed that he would never attend a funeral again. (Funeral and cemetery, in fact, became a motif in his films: in *Stolen Kisses*, *The Man Who Loved Women* and *The Green Room*). At his mother's funeral he was helped by his friend Helen Scott, a tough New Yorker ('my armour-plated protector') who interpreted for him during the long interviewing sessions with Alfred Hitchcock which were written up for his book on the classic director, always one of Truffaut's 'great tutelary figures'. After the funeral Truffaut had an immediate duty to take care of Janine's possessions, and at her apartment in the Rue de Navarin he made a discovery which made him think deeply about his own history and faced him with the kind of materials to which he responded, or was increasingly responding, as an artist. At the apartment there was a wealth of papers recording his own career, a cache of which he had been ignorant. He had never known his mother was interested in him and it was a revelation. Janine had followed his life at a distance. There were many of his own things in the apartment: childhood diaries, school exercise-books, teenage letters, documents relating to his military service and his period Absent Without Leave from the military and his arrest. Truffaut collected and moved the papers. He sorted them into the folders that remain today at the offices of Les Films de Carrosse and which were used by his biographers. They studied the files called '*My Childhood*', '*My*

Army Life', 'My Articles', 'My Films', 'My Women', 'My
Friends', which made the basis for a collection Truffaut cate-
gorised in his head as 'My Life'. He did think of writing an
autobiography, and in a sense did in a book with characteristic
contents and title, *The Films in My Life*, eventually published in
1975.* Did his discoveries at the Rue de Navarin and his
experience of Janine's funeral produce psychological change
in Truffaut, new understandings which could inform his films?
Perhaps: but what is most clear is the huge effect on Truffaut of
the sheer extent of the materials he found, the documentation,
the process of discovery and research. Truffaut has been ac-
counted a 'literary' film director and he was always engaged
with literature. But he was also 'literary' in a simple, drastic sense
because he was concerned with what might be called the letters
of experience: the *papers* which are paradoxically both intimate
and enigmatic. His discoveries after the death of Janine provoked his fascination with documents, a fascination which was
leading him back to Roché's documentary novel, *Two English
Girls and the Continent*. Also, something happened not long
before the death of his mother that set him on this path.

Stolen Kisses, begun early in 1968, was the second full-length
film about Antoine Doinel, now a young man recently ejected
from the army and in love with a charming young music student
(Christine Darbon). He takes odd jobs in Paris and one of them
is for a detective agency, a useful narrative trick because it gives
Antoine a ticket to a myriad of situations, sad and funny, around
which the story is constructed. The film is essentially one about
romance, obsessions and about Paris; it has its moral shocks,
and a strange but touching blankness in its ending, but it does
not appear to have issued out of introspection. Truffaut was,
though, ready for some psychological review. He had done his
research into Parisian investigation bureaux, basing the one in
the film, 'Agence Blady', on a real-life Agence Dubly. At the end
of the shoot Truffaut commissioned the agency director, Albert
Duchenne, to find his natural father. Duchenne duly came up

---

* The title was a homage to Henry Miller's *The Books in My Life*. For another
way in which Miller was important to Truffaut, p. 194.

with the name of Roland Lévy, a Jewish dentist who had left Paris for the Swiss border and Belfort at the time of German occupation. The fact that Lévy was Jewish aroused Truffaut. He once said he had always felt himself to be Jewish. (When Truffaut tried to trace Lévy, the family spurned his inquiries about why Roland left Janine: the only family member who did reply denied indignantly that Roland was frozen out because he was Jewish.)

Roland Lévy apparently lived in Boulevard Carnot in Belfort. According to Truffaut's biographers (through Suzanne Schiffman remembers somewhat differently), in September 1968 Truffaut paid a visit to the block of post-war flats from which, he had been told, Lévy emerged each day for an early evening constitutional. At seven o'clock Truffaut stationed himself across the street: at half-past the hour a stout man in his sixties appeared, wrapped in a grey topcoat wearing a silk foulard (as Truffaut does in many photographs). Truffaut watched – and retreated. He then took a hotel room and spent the remainder of the evening in a cinema, watching Chaplin's *The Gold Rush*. He returned to Paris the next day, without completing his mission.

We know about Truffaut's aborted encounter in Belfort from his biographers who studied the Truffaut papers at Les Films de Carrosse. They mention one intriguing scrap of paper in the collection, a map of Belfort on which the route between the station and the Boulevard Carnot is carefully inked in. Not a surprising item considering the mission that Truffaut was planning. But there is a thread which links this functional document with Truffaut's artistry and his sense of himself. Two years earlier he had directed in England his version of Ray Bradbury's *Fahrenheit 451*. Bradbury's novel is about a dystopia in which books and reading are banned, so an underground movement of refugees resists the state and secures the survival of writing by committing books to memory after which they are destroyed, each rebel 'becoming' the book by whose name she or he is known. The leader of one chapter (not a pun made in the film) of book-people is *The Life of Henry Brulard* by

Stendhal. One commentator has called the book the 'most visual of all autobiographies', which is not to say that it is a picture-book, but it is a book full of sketch-maps on which are inscribed inked legends: it is a volume, but it is also a note-book.* And Truffaut's map of Belfort indeed resembles one of its pages – say,

> There I was born; this house belonged to my father, who sold it when he started building his new street and committing follies. The street that ruined him he named the Rue Dauphin (my father was an extreme *ultra*, on the side of the priests and nobles) and is nowadays called, I believe, the *Rue La Fayette*. I have spent my life at my grandfather's, whose house was hardly more than a hundred paces from our own . . .

. . . near which is a diagram of part of the town of Grenoble in 1793, with the father's house indicated, a subsequent map showing the location of Brulard's grandfather's house in the Place Grenette. (Like Truffaut, he was reared in a grandparental home.) The documentary presence in the text is both exact and enigmatic, and relates to Truffaut's map: one imagines him (poet in the afternoon) doodling it *à la* Stendhal. Text-creation, diary-making, and documentation was on his mind. He had been through his mother's collection, he knew the Roché's hoard of papers, including the *Carnets*, he remembered that Roché's second novel was made like an album out of dozens of scraps, testimony to the desire of Pierre and Margaret to set on record the efforts of their hearts. He was moving back into the orbit of *Two English Girls and the Continent*. But Truffaut's main preoccupation in the late 1960s was the new security he had found with Catherine Deneuve.

Although *Mississippi Mermaid* (in which Deneuve starred) did not perform well at the box-office, two 'small' pictures of

---

* 'Henry' in the title of Stendhal's novel is correct – Truffaut's (and Roché's) penchant for the English language is in tune with it. It is John Sturrock who called it a 'visual novel' in the introduction to his translation of it for Penguin Classics.

1969–1970, *The Wild Child* and *Bed and Board* (which explored the married life of Antoine Doinel and Christine Darbon), were profitable. At the end of the 1960s Deneuve and Truffaut were looking forward to a period of refreshment. She was planning a year away from acting and he wanted to recharge his batteries, having made four films in two years – though to decide against making a film was ominously against type for Truffaut. The couple said at last they would have all the time they wanted for each other because they had no film commitments after Christmas 1970. Truffaut wanted to write more: he decided to edit a book of his film reviews and write introductions to pieces by his mentors, André Bazin and Sacha Guitry. This somewhat valetudinarian plan faltered. And Truffaut's union with Catherine collapsed.

Truffaut's biographers surmise that the couple quarrelled over Catherine's desire for another child. At the end of November 1970 she told Truffaut she wanted to cut short their holiday in Tunisia. They returned to Paris together, where they separated. Catherine left for a winter sports resort with her son, Christian, and Truffaut abandoned their apartment for the Hôtel George V. He closeted himself in a fifth-floor suite and then decamped to rooms in the building where the office of Les Films de Carrosse was located. His friends had never seen him so desperate. Jeanne Moreau insisted he had medical treatment, so he was taken to Dr René Held, an elderly specialist in the medication of psychosomatic conditions, who recommended a sleep cure of a kind today considered dangerous. Truffaut was admitted to the Clinique Villa-des-Pages at Vésinet near Versailles. 'The colours of my pills are my only horizon,' he said. He took only one book with him, *Two English Girls and the Continent*, and, when conscious, read and re-read it, and continued to do so after leaving the clinic in a daze. All his film production business had been handed over to Marcel Berbert, his company secretary, a familiar face from small parts in Truffaut films, playing sober businessmen or officials. Truffaut suffered from mood swings and nightmares as he waited for Catherine to telephone, smoking even more cigarettes than usual.

Immediately after his hospitalisation he decided he must make a film and that it had to be his version of *Two English Girls and the Continent*. Work progressed fast: psychologically, Truffaut needed it to move. Thanks to the success of *The Wild Child* and *Bed and Board* it was possible to raise money quickly from an independent producer-distributor, Hercule Mucchielli, with a guarantee of 400,000 dollars for US distribution from Columbia. Truffaut already had a script for *Anne and Muriel* from Jean Gruault – but one which he had shelved because it was too long, and now, to make matters more difficult, he wanted to incorporate even more material into the film, some from the *Carnets* and some from his background reading. He and Gruault were immersing themselves in 'the wonderful Brontë sisters', as Truffaut called them, and in Marcel Proust. They said they wanted a film to be about Proust in love with Charlotte Brontë. Truffaut was haunted by an anecdote he had heard about Emily Brontë: when she was dying she said, 'I can taste the earth in my mouth.' Truffaut and Gruault attacked the lengthy draft screenplay for *Anne and Muriel* and, by the use of whisky and scissors, reduced it to a manageable half of its length.

The shoot of *Anne and Muriel* took place between May and July 1971. Suzanne Schiffman, Truffaut's long-time collaborator, went to London to cast the four main English rôles and engaged, for the sisters, two young actresses, unknown to his films and unfamiliar with cinema work. Anne was to be played by Kika Markham, and Muriel by Stacey Tendeter who had just left drama school. Truffaut had actually thought of having real sisters to play the English girls, but not surprisingly this did not work out. The other British actors engaged in London played Mrs Brown (Mrs Court) and the friend of the family, Mr Flint (Mr Dale), who organised the separation of Claude and Muriel. Claude was to be played by Jean-Pierre Léaud, now established as Antoine Doinel or pseudo-Truffaut in three films. *Anne and Muriel* was to show a new Léaud, more subdued than in the Doinel cycle and so diffident in manner that Stacey Tendeter wondered why the English girls were so attracted to such a passive man, lacking in presence. He even looked taller as Antoine Doinel, and in *Anne and Muriel* he laughs only once. Léaud had recently lost a woman friend and Truffaut sometimes urged him to keep the grief out of his face. The result was a deference in his performance, selflessly attained by the actor, which enhanced the spectacle of the sisters' power.*

Although he could not have real sisters for the girls, Truffaut did, once shooting had started, actually engage the father of Kika Markham for the film. David Markham plays the palmist who is consulted by the sisters and promises emotional prosperity for Muriel: 'You will be engaged to one man twice.' He hesitantly admires Anne, saying in English, 'You will love several men. You don't care what the world thinks.' When he looks more closely at her palm, it is clear to the audience, though not to Anne, that he is frightened: 'There's great danger here. You should take care of yourself.' Typically for Truffaut, who liked to cast actors against expectation, there is nothing ominous about this fortune-teller: a gentle, handsome and prematurely white-haired man in a well-cut suit, who looks like a family friend. The playing of this scene by father and daughter had a resonance for the actors because by the time it was shot Kika Markham had begun a love affair with Truffaut of which David Markham was aware – indeed, he first met Truffaut over dinner in Paris, when he was visiting his daughter, and Truffaut liked him so much that he gave him a part. Suzanne Schiffman gently reminded Kika Markham of what Truffaut himself admitted in more than one interview: that he was always very drawn to the parents of a woman he was going out with, especially the fathers.

As the filming progressed, she became less of the nervous tomboy, and members of the crew noticed that Truffaut was

---

* Compare Léaud's diffident performance to a similar one, equally good: Tom Cruise's wrongly vilified performance as Bill Harford in Stanley Kubrick's *Eyes Wide Shut*. In this film, as in *Anne and Muriel*, the male lead is seemingly shallow, surrounded by the passion in the female leads.

more like the self they knew before the rupture with Catherine Deneuve. It is tempting to relate her effect on Truffaut to the moment in *Anne and Muriel* when Anne prompts Claude in a sculpture arcade to drop the cane he had been using and make his way unaided; he does so, manifestly proud of his recovery, and Anne follows half a pace behind him, holding the cane in both hands behind her back, like a young lieutenant.

But there were sadnesses for Kika Markham during and after the shoot. It could be lonely to be 'put up on the screen again' as an actress after sharing time with her director as lover in a hotel. She was immersed in left-wing politics and tried to start a debate with Truffaut about Marx and, especially, Trotsky, which was difficult in her fair but unpractised French. The presence of her father did not make matters easier. Truffaut liked him very much: he was 'the father of all fathers,' she later said rather ruefully. After *Anne and Muriel* was finished it was father rather than daughter who was engaged to play a part in Truffaut's forthcoming picture about the film-making process. In *Day for Night* David Markham plays a father figure, the doctor husband of a young film star, a part which Kika Markham would have dearly liked. She visited Truffaut at Antibes when he was preparing the film and was disappointed to hear that there was to be no part for her in the new project. She later wrote that

> he had wanted to give her a farewell present. He owned some beautiful old watches, but she was too proud to accept one (although she later regretted this). In the end she chose his old yellow towel bathrobe because it was the only scruffy thing he owned and it comforted her. He promised to write and hoped she wouldn't be too sad . . .*

* From one of two stories, not yet published, by Kika Markham about her *Anne and Muriel*.

They had done some sketches and she had Truffaut's, of which this picture is one. *Anne and Muriel* was edited by late August 1971, a phenomenally fast completion. Its final length was 134 minutes. Although this was long for a film of that time, there were reasonably good reports from the first private screenings. Truffaut received warm messages from his friends, who commented especially on its intimacy. Denise Roché said that she felt that throughout its length Henri Pierre Roché had been at her side. The film was premièred in November – but then the response of the critics was what Truffaut's biographers call 'catastrophique'. Box-office receipts were bad. The critics were indignant, finding the film clumsy, even vulgar (the 'deflowering' of Muriel). The performance of Jean-Pierre Léaud, pushed this way and that by the sisters, was seen as comic by some reviewers. Truffaut was a modest director who respected both the critics and the public, so he tried to mend matters. At first he thought impulsively of revising the film and drastically abandoning material, but Suzanne Schiffman pleaded with him not to cut the negative. Instead he produced a version shorter by fourteen minutes and considered showing the original in some cinemas and a shorter version in others. The film fared better outside France, but it never became popular. Truffaut travelled to give *Anne and Muriel* publicity. In Canada he was interviewed at length for television, revealing things, he said, of which he had never spoken before and of which he would never speak again. He spent Christmas 1971 in Athens with his ex-wife Madeleine and their daughters: a happy interlude.

The critics thought *Anne and Muriel* was 'not Truffaut', meaning it lacked dash or humour or was not 'cinematic'. Although the film is a good-looking one and Truffaut rightly told his brilliant cinematographer, Nestor Almendros, that there was not an ugly frame in it, these frames are rather staid: indeed, it could be said to be a film of frames or sets ('bourgeois drawing-room', 'bohemian café') without the kinetic energy that was expected from Truffaut. One episode was popular: Claude and Anne's holiday, when they have sex for the first time, was felt to be securely Truffaut-like, 'French' and up-to-date. The final moment of this episode is

indeed charming, when Anne and Claude leave their island hide-
away in dinghies, resolutely rowing away from each other, to the
left and right of the screen, *copain* back-packers to the last minute
of their vacation. This cheery scene was applauded, but the
harrowing ones derided, like Muriel's confession, made straight
to a camera which advances upon her until only her eyes are
visible. The film was painfully sincere, did not flatter the audience
by being 'like Hitchcock', and was not sweet, not the work of
'Truffaut la tendresse' as he was either admiringly or sarcastically
called and whose *Stolen Kisses* had its very title taken from a
quirkily nostalgic song by Charles Trenet. *Anne and Muriel* was
clearly not a dull film: it was seen to have some of the weird
urgency of Hitchcock's *Vertigo*, but it was set perhaps over-
picturesquely in the *belle époque* and Edwardian periods and
lacked the mystery element which made *Vertigo* compelling. The
critics thought it wordy and its length was troubling.

Truffaut was convinced that *Anne and Muriel* did not work
with the critics because it was not shown at its full length. He
may have been right: in the versions that became current there
were unexpected jumps in the narrative. In September 1983,
when he was settling his affairs before he entered hospital for an
operation after a cerebral haemorrhage, he said that *Anne and
Muriel* was 'my only film that was massacred, amputated,
truncated'. He wanted it restored to its original length. Only
after his death was a proper print prepared. Why did such a
business-like director believe that 134 minutes would be acceptable to audiences? There was something strange about his
conviction that the film would have succeeded at its original
length because he had actually never made a film as long as that.
With the exception of *Mississippi Mermaid*, a critical failure, all
his previous films were less than two hours long. It is understandable that he wanted a 'director's cut', as it was later called.*

---

* *Anne and Muriel* can now be seen at its full length, thanks to a restoration in
laser-disc format by the US company, Voyager. A printed text appeared in January
1972, soon after the film itself, in the periodical *L'Avant-Scène Cinéma*, which
gives material from the full-length film and parts of the original screenplay which
were never shot. There is also some material which was photographed but not
included in the full version.

If Truffaut was disappointed to see his film shortened, Roché would probably have been bewildered to see so much of his material missing. It might have been difficult to maintain cordial relations with his young admirer. Truffaut always made elliptical films, so not surprisingly there is no ordinary substantiation of character or scene-setting: the artistic Anne is never seen at art-school nor the studious Muriel with her books. But there are more radical elisions. Everything connected with London life, including the involvement of Claude/Pierre and Muriel/Margaret with poverty and the East End and their ideological arguments about it, is missing. *Anne and Muriel* never shows how closely Pierre and Margaret were bound together emotionally after Pierre's proposal, in spite of Margaret's rejection of him, and it does not show what really happened after Pierre meekly left Margaret in the Kent countryside at the end of May 1902. In Truffaut's version he rather banally leaves for Paris where he finds the delights of independent women. He is cheerfully led into an affair with Ruta, who makes postcard pictures for lovers and soldiers and shows Claude a nude painting of herself, and he has another affair with a Monique Montferrand (the surname of Truffaut's mother) whom Mme Roché is delighted to meet when she encounters her. Monique is flushed from an embrace with Mme Roché's son, who has now clearly established himself with 'satisfactory' Parisiennes, rather than gauche, demanding English girls. Claude soon becomes active in the world of art. Mme Roché is proud to see his first article in a journal ('La Reprise de *Salomé* à l'Oeuvre'). He begins to travel and purchase paintings for a collector. It is hard to tell whether Truffaut meant it, but Claude very quickly acquires the patina of a Bond Street dealer, suited and deferential. Roché himself was well-dressed, but Truffaut's Claude appears to belong to the auction house rather than the studio, not easily imagined at Toulka's 'little orgy' or introducing Picasso to Gertrude Stein, or enjoying the company of John Quinn.

In *Anne and Muriel* Claude is not presented as any kind of thinker; Nietszche is never mentioned. Claude rather suddenly

becomes a writer, though the subject of his book has no connection at all with his experiences with the sisters. It is called
Jerôme and Julien, an equivalent obviously to *Jules and Jim*, but
there is in the film no friendship between a Roché-figure and a
Franz/Jim-figure. In reality it was Margaret who died young,
though long after the dissolution of the trio and her relationship
with Pierre. She survives in the novel and in the film. In reality
and in the novel Violet/Anne, after the main action, embarked on
a happy life. But in the film Anne falls ill, reunites with Max-
Diurka, but dies with the apocryphal words of Emily Brontë ('I
can taste the earth in my mouth') on her lips.

It is easy to find reasons for Truffaut's abbreviation and
alteration of his sources. An obvious one was practical. He
was determined to make a film with therapeutic speed. He had to
shorten an unwieldy screenplay. To show Anne and Muriel's
London life would have raised logistical and financial problems.
Also, drastic abbreviation enabled him to make a film very
different from the (predominantly) cheerful *Jules and Jim*. It
had to have a different pace: even jerkiness was acceptable in a
film with so much talking – to shake about, as it were, the
conversations. He was absorbed by Roché's novel, but not
slavish: and he wanted to make a *violent* film, not, in Roché's
phrase, 'a gentle story of three friends'.

If Truffaut became fascinated by archives, his own and Roché's,
in the late 1960s, what connection is there between this fascination and *Anne and Muriel*? There is an obvious one in the style
Truffaut used for the credit titles of his film. The titles remind us
that we are to see an adaptation of a book, but in a very different
way from the cinema's conventional genuflection to the literary
work. The old-fashioned Hollywood beginning shows a simu-
lacrum of a book, perhaps with a title-page vignette that 'comes
to life'. This does not happen in *Anne and Muriel* which shows
us straight away and successively the front cover of the Gallimard edition of the novel, then some pages which have scribbled
notes on them, surely Truffaut's, written in the clinic at Vésinet.
One of these annotations is a cross-reference to Roché's journal,

a source which we, the audience, have no way of accessing. Then we see pages, text but in *pages*, one after another. We only see cross-chapter openings, except in one case when we see (an unusual feature of Roché's novel) the page openings where the prose is segmented into two columns, making simultaneous narrative. We also see multiple copies. Imprinted on these shots is letterpress giving names of the film-making personnel. The effect is the opposite of the conventional 'literary' opening. There is no sign of the novel being 'opened out'. We are not drawn in by these sights, nor are we drawn in by the arrival of the voice-over commentary:

> Tonight, I again lived over our story in detail. One day I will make a book. Muriel thought that an account of our difficulties would be useful to others.

The enunciation is so precise, so fast, that it sounds as if the speaker were reading from an autocue. We are soon to know this urgent, reedy, desperate-sounding voice is that of Claude and it is reasonable to think this male protagonist is dictating his story, which maintains the distance, keeping us (as it were) out of the frame of the past, an effect enhanced by the fact that the film is 'macaronic', that is, in two languages, the characters shifting between French and English, with awkward language-use in the foreign speakers. No film director has ever been as sensitive as François Truffaut to what could be called cross-languaging in his film. (The subject arises in his own appearance in 1977 as a French scientist with awkward English in Spielberg's *Close Encounters of the Third Kind*.) All these phenomena are confrontational. And physical. They point to the fact that we are about to see a strange version of a novel.

Two English Girls and the Continent is not a complicated or dense narrative work, hard for an adapter to boil down into a screenplay. It is a swift read and there is no density of narration – indeed, there is no narration except what is told by the protagonists. It is a book of documents, and the experience of studying the surviving Roché and Court papers is not so very different from reading the novel that Roché wrote about himself and the girls. None the less *Anne and Muriel*, this confrontational work, simplifies the novel in the roughest of ways: the survivor Anne is killed off (childless), much discussion is eliminated (even in the earliest version), and whole tracts of the characters' experience removed (Claude's in England, Muriel's in France). Is it a travesty or a distillation?

If not a distillation, it is an essay *in* or *at* Roché's novel, a kind of *poem* deriving from Roché. There are positive aesthetic reasons for the blatancy of Truffaut's adaptation, for wrenching a documentary novel into the form of a melodrama. I guess that Truffaut wanted certain peaks, and felt, as poets sometimes feel, that a work is to be made for certain moments, its superstructure devised for the sake of them. A critic once said that Shakespeare wrote *Macbeth* in order to have the sight of a 'Bloody Child' on the stage: he wrote the play around it, to accommodate his desire.* Truffaut did not want fidelity in the usual sense. One might see him, contrariwise, giving out this film as if it were a set of poems inspired by a legend. And he was, anyway, in a hurry. I suggest *Anne and Muriel* was made for certain moments and that one of them was Muriel's confession. On this confession let us focus, after a word on the events in the film which lead up to it.

When he was planning his novel Roché made, we saw earlier, a three-column diagram listing the qualities of Claude, Anne and Muriel. In the Muriel column he wrote 'Young Prophetess'. One feels this in *Anne and Muriel*, with Muriel as seer, though at first the blind one, a figure from an old world, compared to the friendly Anne with her gift for intimacy. Our first sighting is when Anne brings Claude down to meet Muriel for the first time at the supper-table. She has, of course, straight red hair to her shoulders, her face looking the longer because of a crêpe bandage round her eyes and forehead, the edge of which she raises to see her plate and Claude. The bandage is soon replaced

---

* See a wonderful book of 1936, G. Wilson Knight's *Principles of Shakespearean Production, with especial reference to the Tragedies.*

by black-tinted spectacles, so memorably present when she looks on darkly at Anne giving Claude the 'nun's kiss' as a forfeit through the bars of the Windsor chair in the yellow firelight. We become especially conscious of her eyes, for instance, addressing herself to her bedroom mirror, to which she intones that 'I will *not* be jealous of my sister.' Truffaut liked the device of an actor talking to a mirror: love-sick Antoine Doinel performs the same act in *Stolen Kisses*. (Were *Anne and Muriel* an opera, this would be the basis of a first-act aria for Muriel.) Muriel does laugh sometimes, more so than Anne, in fact. One night she goes downstairs to find Claude alone, after which they go up to their rooms together. On the top landing he touches her hand, and then, intensely, raises his hand to her face with a sort of framing gesture. 'Why did you do that?' 'Because you come from the earth and that delights me.' 'It is time to go to sleep,' says Muriel with the little laugh she uses when she says, with charming pomposity, that we cannot know virtue if we know nothing of vice, after Claude has explained French prostitution to the wide-eyed sisters.

The laughter occurs before the couple are separated, immediately after which Muriel's suffering starts, taking the form of a miniature version of Truffaut's film of 1975, *The Story of Adèle H.*, about the obsession of the daughter of Victor Hugo with a young military officer she met in Jersey, who had flirted effectively but callously. When posted to Nova Scotia, Adèle follows him, trying every desperate method of securing his attention. Muriel is seen, like Adèle, talking to herself in the street. A policeman, played by Truffaut, looks round in astonishment at her. Life then becomes worse for Muriel, as we know, when Claude/Pierre decides to cancel the arrangement imposed on them. In *Anne and Muriel* he writes as follows (in French):

Dear Muriel,
I need to be alone for what I want to do. I will not be returning to England at the moment. I will be in central Europe to look at paintings. I will be writing about them, and translating. It is necessary for me to live without wife and child. This should

console you. I have woman friends, but I have decided not to marry. I think I will be able to live without my sisters, but they will be neither forgotten nor replaced. We will exchange letters back and forth, but if you wish for an untroubled life, we must say good-bye.

Your brother,

Claude.

Claude shows this frigid epistle to his mother before posting it: the audience hears it as Mme Roché reads. Muriel opens it in Wales and collapses on the green sward (melodrama, indeed) outside the Browns' cottage. Scenes follow which culminate in her mental collapse and confinement to bed from which she awakens to welcome darkness, and says in French, 'I want all of Claude or nothing. If nothing, then let it be death', and in English, 'I'm no longer going to write this diary for Claude. It's monotonous. If I do write one, it will be for myself.' After which comes her astounding confession, important in Chapter XIII of the novel and surely the heart of the film. This is one of the passages for which I think the film was made: one of its *raisons d'être*.

We see the sisters in Wales. Muriel hands Anne a parcel for the post: 'The last thing I shall ever send him.' In Paris, Claude looks at it, recognising the handwriting. The wrapping gives way to reveal an exercise-book marked as being Muriel's journal, and also a letter which Claude takes out. The voice-over says that Claude is receiving 'part of her journal, a confession'. We see Muriel's face and, in a close-up which comes increasingly, even oppressively or sadistically, closer, she makes an impassioned statement to Claude and us. This shot is interrupted by very brief shots, but longer than flash-shots, showing some things happening as she recounts them. We see, too, the text of a letter from an American Christian organisation which advised Muriel and from which she quotes.

It should be remembered that what Claude receives is a journal, and that the confession is part of a journal, and that the confession 'stands for' a journal. It is possible to miss this in the speed of the moment. Muriel warns Claude that she has a confession and he will see that 'we are quits'. ('Attention: préparez-vous à lire ma confession et vous verrez que nous sommes quittés.') She tells him she learned how to touch herself for pleasure at the age of eight, from a girl-friend, Clarisse, and she continued to find masturbating irresistible up to the age of seventeen, and perhaps longer, possibly to the present: she does not say. She wants Claude to know she is no longer pure (not 'une fille intacte'), but is weakened in body and mind. Claude is her friend, so she *has to* tell him.

The confession is segmented. It begins with the revelation of uncleanness which she learned, she says, from a pamphlet or 'brochure' (in French), not a book. But she says that she had already felt guilt even before the revelation. She accuses herself, backed by shots of Clarisse, the 'corrupter', and of herself alone, lying down to pleasure herself on a hot day. This set of flashbacks forms a mini-film, as it were, within the confession episode of *Anne and Muriel*, breaking in upon Muriel's torrential address to Claude and the film's audience. The children, Muriel and Clarisse, laughing and smiling, first roam along a yellow gorse-covered hillside, above the Browns' cottage, then roll down it, then play with dolls, then they are in bed, with Clarisse struggling out of her night-dress and embracing; then there is Muriel alone at the age of seventeen throwing herself restlessly down in the sun, raising her skirt in the heat; then there is Muriel in bed, aroused, perhaps, in her sleep. This segment of film-within-film is like thick painted colour across the spoken confession, streaks of paint which orient everything else to them.

We also see the advice that Muriel sought in the form of a letter under this heading (of which Roché had a typographic facsimile in his Chapter XIII).

LEAGUE OF CHRISTIAN WOMEN OF AMERICA
PURITY SECTION

The writer sympathises, but tells Muriel to waste no time on self-reproach: she must throw herself into an active, outdoor life. She must acknowledge that she has learned how to do something disgusting ('nocif'). Even if it happens in sleep she must promise to wash in a cold bath when she wakes. The writer is kindly, severe and positive: the practice must be quelled by discipline, a healthy life and hydropathic, respiratory, and digestive treatments. She must look to the future.*

The series of flashbacks is vertiginous, but so is the confessional episode as a whole: and it is not too much to say that it is frightening. Some people have found it cruel, the camera driving closer and closer to the face of Muriel, like the deadly tripod-bayonet in Michael Powell's horrible film *Peeping Tom*. In *Anne and Muriel* the advancing camera is fended off (so to speak) by the language Muriel delivers at it, at Claude, at oneself and at herself, too, because she is speaking – as we have already seen – to her mirror. Muriel downloads her anguish and embarrasses the medium, the story-telling medium of film with its basic mode of identification, flickering shot-by-shot between characters, an especially decorous medium in the case of the period film. It is tempting to say that the film 'crashes' at this point and in one way it does: it refuses to let the audience do the interpreting that in other circumstances would beckon. The cascading method does make us think one thing about Muriel: that she is not a trapped creature, and that she has found not perhaps *her* sexuality, but *a* sexuality. The method also successfully stops us thinking at least two things, one moralistic and one erotic.

What Muriel says in this sequence is what she says in Roché's novel, that she has enjoyed masturbating, that she learned how bad it was, a badness recognised by the League of Christian

* On the presence of this letter in Roché's novel, see Chapter Two, 'Will it be terrible, or nothing at all?', p. 79. There is an intriguing difference between the letter in the film and in the novel. In the film the letter-headed address of the League of Christian Women is the same, with the addition of 'Little Rock: Ark.' Why should Truffaut have made this change? One wonders whether he had seen the real letter in some papers of Roché now lost, a letter whose address the novelist abbreviated. A further curiosity is that Little Rock, Arkansas was the home of President Bill Clinton who in 1994 dismissed Surgeon General Joycelyn Elders for advocating masturbation for young people in the press and in her book, *The Dreaded 'M' Word*.

Women of America which admonishes and advises, and she says all this to Claude. Even in 1971 it was unlikely that the audience would respond moralistically to Muriel's confession as did the League of Christian Women. But it could have reacted moralistically to the League's letter and to Muriel's environment by thinking 'poor Muriel', afflicted by archaic taboos. Truffaut took this risk when he allowed the League to advise cold baths, long known as a comically out-of-touch palliative. The 'poor Muriel' response would place her as victim and pleasingly assure the audience of its own, post-1960s, enlightenment, as if looking down and back on the dark ages of repression. As for the fact that Muriel is addressing her confession to Claude, here the moralistic response could be reproof at her for manipulatively 'making him feel guilty', a serious crime in the liberal register. The torrentiality, the overload, aesthetically defuses these banalities: the audience is left no mental space for such dear moralisms. Nor is the audience left room for an erotic response. Part of Muriel's confession is the revelation of her sexual education by Clarisse, when aged eight, which has potential for an erotic response on the part of the audience, or sectors of it. Is voyeurism invited? Watching women masturbate is a traditional male erotic fad, with or without awareness of it by women. (In the late 1990s Leland Elliott and Cynthia Brantley's *Sex on Campus* interestingly reported that 32 percent of young campus women 'had masturbated in front of someone'.) In this case the style, the drive to explain in the words and the tumbling figures on the screen, make reactive participation impossible.

After the confession we see Claude considering its impact in a chamber as shrouded as a funeral parlour and hear from the voice-over that 'Muriel's confession provoked in Claude more curiosity than emotion.' The reaction is unsettlingly dispassionate, especially that 'most of all, he dreamt of the literary work he could make out of it.' The voice goes on to say that he asked Muriel for permission to publish her confession and that she refused. We then see Claude dictating Muriel's words (some of which we have heard already in her voice) to a female stenographer at a typewriter. He paces the room, his voice rising to an almost theatrical boom, giving the female stenographer an interested look, none of which is endearing. In *Two English Girls and the Continent* Roché is quietly observant: it will be remembered that he appends a footnote to Muriel's confession which directs the reader to part of Pierre's journal in which he describes a rapturous moment in the Alps in which *he* masturbates and ejaculates ('gives himself') to the sunrise. He is unpassionate, not so austere as Truffaut's Claude: the footnote makes a parallel between the experience of Pierre/Claude and Muriel, a sad parallel.* But we have to arrest a thought of callousness in Claude. If he had not dictated Muriel's confession, there would have been no book. The perils of being an *informateur* are exposed. The point is not so much that Claude is unattractive in this episode, 'exploiting' Muriel, but that he is a nullity, literally not evaluatively so. He is the channel down which the data passes to us, the one who turns Muriel's torrent into markings on a page and movements on a screen. Truffaut had to take pains to keep Claude back as a personality and Jean-Pierre Léaud selflessly helped him. At the beginning of the film he did say, 'Tonight, I again lived over our story in detail. One day I will make a book. Muriel thought that an account of our difficulties would be useful to others.' Truffaut wanted to show us something and make us curious about it. Just as Roché dispassionately was.

What of the aftermath of the confession, the last act in the friendship of Claude and the 'Young Prophetess'? We see Claude in Paris buttonholed by Diurka, Anne's former lover. He says he knows Muriel will be going to Brussels as a teacher (like Charlotte Brontë): she could be met at Calais, he says, and Claude hurries there to see Muriel at the quay. Muriel allows him to stay at her hotel as if expecting him. She is carefully dressed, with hair up and spectacles, in governess style. She enters Claude's rooms and they make love passionately, seven years after their first meeting in Wales. Muriel is thirty, but looks twenty. 'She is like snow in his hands,' says the voice-over which

* See Chapter Three, p. 84.

continues during the passage of sex, though some of the spoken commentary from the script is missing from the film. Muriel's hymen gives more easily than Anne's, and, after Claude has penetrated her, the screen fills with the blood that is on their bed sheet. There is none of the happiness of the 'three days' episode in *Two English Girls and the Continent*, only blood on a sheet. It was not, says the commentary, a matter of happiness, nor of tenderness. 'It was a matter of Claude arming Muriel the woman against himself.'

In the morning Muriel makes to leave; Claude is surprised, now wanting to stay with her, and knowing she could bear their child. Muriel explains seriously that there is no place for children in his life. 'You can become more useful in your work than with children,' and 'Now I know love, I can live without you, as one can live without eyes, or limbs.' 'We are not', she says in French, 'of the same tribe. We do not have the same ceremonies. I am a loving Puritan, and you love me because you are . . . a little deranged.' Claude sees her depart. A little later he has a letter in Paris from Muriel to say that, yes, a baby is expected. 'This paper is your skin, this ink my blood.' Another letter follows, which should, writes Muriel, have a black border. She is not pregnant, but 'after the night in Calais, we will never again rise so high.'*

François Truffaut entered the life of Henri Pierre Roché and the life he spent with the two English girls. Roché gave him two books to film – and also gave him the other book, his journals, the *Carnets*, so far read by only a handful of people. It was in the *Carnets*, which will be published eventually, that Roché tried to write like Casanova, 'only in a different spirit'. Roché bequeathed a rich fund to Truffaut, so much that no simple influence on his life and art can be docketed. If there is any one element to be stressed, I would choose not the human connections (for instance, loving sisters, English women,

---

* For the end of the story of Muriel in *Anne and Muriel*, see Epilogue, 'The Trio is Over', p. 197.

'Casanova' love-life), but Truffaut's stylistic preoccupation, his pleasure in Roché's text, its roughness or physicality. These pleasures we experience in *Anne and Muriel*. But also, in the end, Truffaut absorbed the *subject* of *Two English Girls and the Continent*: that is, romantic love.

Can it be said that the subject of *Anne and Muriel* is romantic love when its material (the male/sisters triangle) is so out-of-the-way, so arcane? Romantic love does, however, thrive on three features packed into the double overlapping triangles, the entanglement of Claude, Anne and Muriel. These features are transgression, duplication and adoption. First, romantic love transgresses because it feels forbidden: the intact self is vertiginously troubled by the thought of rejection. (This is why romantic love is frequently tongue-tied, something shown with wit in *Four Weddings and a Funeral* – in which the hero's brother is hearing-impaired – and to which is related the two-language – both ill-spoken, or 'macaronic' – quality of *Anne and Muriel*. Mistakes in speech have long been associated with romantic love.) Second, romantic love duplicates because it is always checking the other case against that of the loved one: lovers wonder about what, or who, the loved one is or was (say, as a child) like: how much does the loved one 'owe' to mother or father?* (In the short period in which Pierre Roché was having sex with Violet and intercourse with Margaret seemed in sight, Violet – with typical plain curiosity – asked why he did not find such duplication or familiarity strange. Not at all, he said: it made him want to have sex with their mother as well.) Third, romantic love wants adoption, that is, acceptance by group or tribe by means of erotic application for membership, and usually does not get it, thus the tragedies of romantic love. In romance the beloved is an ambassador from a new tribe, possibly one more materially prosperous, but the prosperity is primarily a symptom of foreignness, even if a new world encrypted in the familiar (the source of much adultery). Truffaut showed in

---

* This aspect of love is explored by James Toback in his 1997 film, *Two Girls and a Guy* – which obviously has Truffaut and Roché in mind: a poster for *Jules and Jim* appears prominently at one point.

Stolen Kisses Antoine Doinel's (and his) disposition to fall in love with a girl-friend's parents; in *Anne and Muriel* the English girls could not be more foreign and Claude is 'The Continent'. The presence of transgression, duplication and adoption in *Anne and Muriel* put it in the great tradition, a modest member of the legendary family of works of art about romantic love: *Romeo and Juliet, Phèdre, Tristan and Isolde*, Henry James's *The Golden Bowl*, as well as various versions of the story of Troilus and Cressida, by Boccaccio, Chaucer, Shakespeare, Robert Henryson and William Walton. A mischievous youthful member of the group is *Lolita* – which was translated into German by Helen Hessel, who was of course wife of Franz, lover of Roché and model for Catherine.

There is another strand in *Anne and Muriel* which relates to Roché and the advice given him early in life to be an 'informateur', or 'investigator'.* No-one ever thought Truffaut a realist, but he was one in that he believed the cinema should be informative – and informative about sex. In 1973, about eighteen months after *Anne and Muriel* was finished, he wrote an essay called 'What Do Critics Dream About?' in which he stated that he believed the cinema had a duty to be sexually explicit. He mentions Henry Miller (whose *The Books in My Life* had inspired his own semi-autobiography, *The Films in My Life*).

> Erotic or pornographic films, without being a passionate fan, I believe . . . are in expiation, or at least in payment of a debt that we owe for sixty years of cinematographic lies about love. I am one of the thousands of his readers who was not only entranced, but helped through life by the work of Henry Miller, and I suffered at the idea that cinema lagged so far behind his books as well as behind reality. Unhappily, I still cannot cite an erotic film that is the equivalent of Henry Miller's writing (the best films, from Bergman to Bertolucci, have been pessimistic, but, after all, freedom for the cinema is still quite new).

*See Chapter One, 'The Trio', p. 11.

Anne and Muriel pays some of the debt by showing what was and is not often seen (hymeneal blood, female masturbation). It joins other films of its era, some of which Truffaut disliked, but which none the less showed people things they wanted to find out about: *Women in Love* (1969), *W.R.: Mysteries of the Organism* (1971), *Last Tango in Paris* (1972) and *Empire of the Senses* (1976). One wonders if there has since been any comparable phase of innovation in the portrayal of sex on the screen. Although there is *Crash* (1997).

In an interview in January 1972, published as 'My Two English Girls: My Eleventh Film' in *L'Avant-Scène: Cinéma* (number 121), Truffaut explained what he wanted from and in *Anne and Muriel*. He said that he wanted to make not a film about physical love, but a physical film about love, that he wanted to show how much suffering was experienced on account of love by young men and women; he said emphatically he wanted to 'squeeze love', the concept of love, 'like a lemon'. At the head of this interview in *L'Avant-Scène* there is a photograph of Truffaut looking through a view-finder and on the side of the camera is pasted a tourist postcard of a Union Jack with a heart imposed. The words 'We Love The British' are printed on to the cross of St George.

Epilogue

the trio is over

The story of the two English girls and Pierre has several endings. Roché gives one of them on the dedication page of *Two English Girls and the Continent* in which we see '*En hommage à Muriel et Anne*' and at the foot of the page, '*Claude (1899–1955)*'. The date 1955 is not, as it first seems, referring to the death of Claude, but to the year in which Roché finished the novel. On this page he is saying farewell to himself as 'Claude'.

The ending of the novel itself is in Chapter XXIII. 'Treize Ans Après', which has two pages of short items: a letter from Anne to Claude and an extract from Claude's journal. Both are dated July 1927 in the novel (the 1st and the 5th), thirteen years later than the previous chapter which has brief letters between Claude and the sisters. Muriel announces that she is about to marry her old friend, who told her that he had always thought that Claude had been in love with 'one of you two sisters'. He thought that if Claude had lived in London, there would have been a wedding. There is nothing, she assures him, to be embarrassed about. Anne writes with snapshots of herself, her husband Ivan, her four children and her sculptures. Thirteen years later she writes from Canada, where the family has settled. We are told that Mme Roc, Claude's mother, is still alive.

So Roché's novel ends more peacefully than Truffaut's film, which is a melodrama – but in a *positive* sense because it deals so directly with the passions of its protagonists, and is perhaps an operatic work with its strong speeches to camera that are like arias.

In Truffaut's film, after the affair with Anne in Paris and the death of his mother, Claude is depressed and listless. He seems to find a way forward by writing his novel, *Jerôme et Julien*, of which we learn nothing, except that it is about a woman who loves two men (not two women who love one man). The connection with *Jules et Jim* is obvious, but there is no connection with Claude in *Anne and Muriel* who has no male friend, no equivalent to Jules or Franz Hessel. Fictional characters do not usually write novels about subjects which have *no* connection with the lives their authors have invented for them. When his novel is in production, Claude encounters Diurka at a printing workshop. Though long parted from Anne, Diurka is still in love with her. Claude knows that Anne is free and back in Wales, having broken off an engagement to a mountain-climber. He tells Diurka who declares he will visit her.

We return to the familiar cottage, outside of which sits a bespectacled Muriel instructing a regimented group of Sunday-school children. Dismissed, they scatter and Muriel takes Diurka to see Anne, who is gravely ill and has been refusing to seek treatment. Diurka immediately proposes marriage and she agrees, saying that she will now consult the doctor whom she spurned. But she has tuberculosis and does not survive. Now we know why the fortune-teller was frightened when he read Anne's palm. We learn that at the end she said, 'I can taste earth in my mouth.' Later in *Anne and Muriel* we see Muriel's three days with Claude, after which she never re-appears. In an 'Epilogue' to the film we hear that the Brown house in Wales is now shut up, letters returned by the post office, and that Muriel is married, with a daughter. Muriel remains, Anne goes.

Why does Truffaut dispose of Anne? What is the logic, narrative, moral or thematic, that informed his decision to eliminate her from his film's fiction? He could have made the decision because of the death of Françoise Dorléac, the sister that died of the two he loved. He may have had Anne die to remind us of the traditional fate of *une Bohème*. Like Puccini's Mimi, Anne has tuberculosis. We know from the screenplay that Truffaut wanted the setting for Anne's Paris attic-studio to be in the old bohemian vein of *La Bohème* or *Trilby*. In any case, artists' attics had not changed much since the 1840s.

There may be other reasons why Anne dies and Muriel survives in *Anne and Muriel*, reasons connected to how varyingly our sympathies work towards and between them. These sympathies can be understood in relation to how we see the sisters' *eyes*. The eyes of both girls are covered in different ways in the course of the film, Anne's with a fashionable *belle époque* net veil at the beginning, and Muriel's with her crêpe bandage. Anne raises her veil gently and exposingly; but there is something remorseless and covert in the sharp eye that appears when Muriel's mask is lifted at the Browns' dinner-table. Anne's death is of a piece with her vulnerability; Muriel's survival signifies what Roché in his first notes for the novel called her 'Napoléonisme'. One is exasperated that in *Anne and Muriel* the prim school-teacher has her way in the end. No wonder the Sunday-school children scattered gratefully after the arrival of Diurka. None of which is to say that either the sympathetic (Anne) or antipathetic (Muriel) impulse wins. They fluctuate and flutter – what Truffaut liked about Edgar Ulmer's *The Naked Dawn* which in 1956 reminded him of *Jules and Jim*'s moral neutrality.

In reality, the story of the two English girls, Violet and Margaret, differed from both novel and film.

On 11 July 1927 Roché went to England on business, though he thought of the journey as the first holiday he had taken for years. He was often seeing Helen Grund, but life with her had become increasingly difficult. Before he left for England they quarrelled over his infidelity, about 'un-existing women', he said to her. They literally fought, as was their way. She knocked over some chess men and then 'got rough' (he wrote in English). She kicked his testicles hard and he hit her face several times. 'Butchery', he wrote in his journal, a word he used for bad boxing. She wept and he nearly fainted. They took a bath. He left soon after for England, with hay-fever, just as he used to have it at this time of year when he was a member in the trio, twenty-five years earlier. The Golden Arrow from Gare du Nord hurried through Kent to London. Roché noticed en route a windmill as the train passed Ashford and he remembered Margaret. In London he accompanied friends on 'quiet lazy jolly marketing in Soho (fruit and vegetables).' The smell of Cuticura hand-cream reminded him of the old English days. He liked Bass beer and sandwiches in 'nice pubs'. He telephoned Violet and learned from her that Margaret was dead. Violet wrote to him on 19 July confirming their conversation, giving the full story of the griefs which had struck the Court family.* She told how Margaret had died the previous year in March, followed soon after by her mother, Emma Court; and, only a fortnight ago, her sister-in-law had gone. Violet added that Margaret's daughter, young Margaret, 'a fine little girl, thoughtful and gentle', now nearly twelve, was attending Bedales, the progressive school in Hampshire. Violet says she will try to find a recent photograph for Pierre. This reference to Margaret's daughter is developed by Roché in *Two English Girls and the Continent*, in which he has Anne write to Claude, saying that young Margaret is to visit Paris and will be in a Paris garden, 'Les Moulages du Trocadéro', on 25 July at 11 o'clock, to which Claude faithfully goes, thinking he recognises the little red-haired girl, called 'Myriam' in the novel, but decides not to approach her.

This is pure fiction: in reality there was no such encounter and of course no such reference in Violet's letter. After receiving it Roché walked around London. He had a veal-and-ham pie at the A.B.C. restaurant at Charing Cross in which he had talked to Margaret years ago. He went up into the National Gallery, as they had done when she had been upset in front of the portrait of Rembrandt's father. (Orphaned of fathers, the children may not like to look at them.) 'I love seeing fine paintings,' Roché said to his diary, a characteristic yet curiously simple remark from one so at home in the world of art. Later, he spent the evening with the painter Ben Nicolson. The next day he had an afternoon with

* See Chapter Four, p. 149, where Violet's letter is quoted.

the plesiosaurs' skeletons at the Natural History Museum in South Kensington.

At the end of *Anne and Muriel* Claude is in the gardens of the Musée Rodin with Rodin's *Balzac* and *The Burghers of Calais* nearby. The voice-over has said that fifteen years have passed, and Muriel is married with a daughter. 'Thousands have died in a war the reasons for which are forgotten. Now Rodin's statue of Balzac is universally admired.' The camera swirls round the exultant, intent figure of the bronze Balzac, a kind of tree-man, above the shoulders of spectators and watched by Claude, who hears English school-girl voices and, when he sees the troupe, wonders if one of them could be young Myriam, daughter of Muriel in the snapshot shown him by Anne in 1899 when she persuaded him to come to England and see her sister for himself. Was that her, the school-girl with red hair? Could he ask? 'It is not worth the trouble.' The girls throng round the entrance to the museum gardens; Claude hurries away and takes a cab.

For some years I remembered this final scene incorrectly. I thought Claude engaged a taxi and, on entering it, saw his reflection in the window, saying in voice-over how old he looked. This does not, of course, happen: one never looks at the window of a cab when opening the door. In fact, the driver refuses Claude, telling him bluntly that he is waiting for someone else, an appropriate device for the film. Claude pauses to look at his reflection in the window of the taxi which will not take him, then walks away.

In Roché's life there was some years later a sighting of 'young Margaret', but an imaginary one. In the spring of 1939 he went to see a stage adaptation of Jules Laforgue's 'Hamlet, or the Consequences of Filial Impiety' and remembered the old days with the Court sisters in Paris, when they read Laforgue together and the girls hated the squashed eyes in the story. They taught him to say 'Oh, my prophetic soul!' in English. On 8 June 1939 he was in the Tuileries and saw, he imagined, 'la fille de Nuk', the phrase carefully placed between quotation marks. This girl was, indeed, in a school party, with the same carriage of her head, 'the same hair, legs, mouth, smile' as Margaret. The breeze made her hat cartwheel along the gravel, stopping at his shoes. 'In the middle of the scene I saw that photo of "Nuk" and remembered all that time when I loved her more than "Mno" and the others.' Seeing duality was always so important for Roché. At the end of *Two English Girls and the Continent* he wrote about the Margaret school-girl in the Rodin gardens.

> I looked at her and I saw Margaret.
> I mingled them together,
> I wanted to take *their* hands.

sources and
acknowledgments

I loved Truffaut's *Anne and Muriel* from its first appearance in 1971 and therefore read and re-read Roché's novel of which I began a translation, until other things intervened. One of these projects took me in 1980 to do research in Texas in one of the great archive collections of the world at the University of Austin, the Harry Ransom Research Center in the Humanities. When it is said that the 'papers went to America' this is often where is meant. I noticed that the Harry Ransom Center had a large collection of Roché's papers and that there had been an exhibition about him, organised by Carlton Lake, book-collector, art critic and curator of French work at the Center. He had been instrumental in acquiring the Roché collection, having known Denise Roché and François Truffaut. Like Truffaut he owned a typescript of the *Carnets*. Lake wrote the best brief account of Henri Pierre Roché in 1975 in one chapter of *Confessions of a Literary Archaeologist*. With Linda Ashton, also of the Harry Ransom Center, he prepared the exhibition catalogue called *Henri-Pierre Roché: An Introduction* (1991), though 'catalogue' does not really do justice to what is effectively an unconventional biography. Instead of arranging entries and illustrations chronologically, as might be expected, Lake and Ashton grouped material under the general headings of 'The Friends' and 'The Works', material that in some cases spans several decades under the name of the friend in question. This was exactly the right procedure for a gregarious, life-loving man, who in a sense subjected himself to friendship, waging a personal campaign against egotism. And each item, especially in the section on *Two English*

Girls and the Continent, was richly annotated by Lake and Ashton.

I learned that Lake and Ashton's exhibition and their *Introduction* only showed the tip of the Roché cache at the Harry Ransom Center, in which there is a mass of material relating to all his literary works, as well as letters and journals and other personal documents. Several files are devoted to *Two English Girls and the Continent*, including drafts, the final typescript, material which was incorporated into the novel and writings by the English girls themselves. These are the files that I used for the writing of this book. I am indebted to Jean-Claude Roché, son of Henri Pierre Roché, for permission to quote from this material, as well as to the surviving family of the English girls.

In *Free Spirits* I have called the English girls 'Margaret and Violet Court', using their real first names but not their real surname. Why? While I was working on the Roché archive some members of the 'Court' family, including the daughters of Margaret and Violet, talked generously and informatively to me about the past. They did not know and were excited to learn that papers of Margaret and Violet are preserved in the Roché archive – excited, and somewhat distressed because, from their vantage-point, the sisters' stories are not happy and were painful to recall. They were worried by the prospect of their family history, or one phase of it, becoming common property as a result of the book I was writing. They knew that the story of Margaret and Violet was on the edge of the public domain: their letters are catalogued at the Harry Ransom Center, their names are in international bibliographical databases, their lives are briefly described in Lake and Ashton's *Introduction* and their family name appears in obituaries of family members. However, it is one thing for researchers to inquire into historical data and another thing for the general public to have access to it through such a book as this. I wanted to write about matters that seemed to me fascinating and important; but I was planning to write about one particularised sector of a family history on which unwelcome public attention could be focused. The 'Court family' could, conceivably, become known for and by one episode in its history, the 'Roché episode', and that could prove distressing. Stéphane Hessel, son of Franz Hessel and Helen Grund (Catherine of *Jules and Jim*), once wrote wryly about people saying to him, 'So you are the little girl in the Truffaut film'. The daughters of Margaret and Violet might become known as the 'daughters of the Two English Girls' and the family name be become identified with a specialised part of its personal history. So I decided it would make sense if the English girls were known as 'Margaret and Violet Court' in *Free Spirits*.

Free Spirits is about Roché and the 'Courts', but of course it is also about Truffaut's film, and in my account of its evolution I have been helped by guidance from the performers who played Muriel (Stacey Tendeter) and Anne (Kika Markham). Ms Markham in particular studied my drafts with an exemplary thoughtfulness: I wish I could have done better justice to her memories and ideas.

Anyone who wishes to explore the territory sketched in *Free Spirits* will want to read *François Truffaut* by Antoine de Baecque and Serge Toubiana (Gallimard, 1996) and *Henri-Pierre Roché: L'Enchanteur Collectionneur* by Scarlett and Philippe Reliquet (Editions Ramsay, 1999), and will want, most of all, the editions of Roché in course of publication by André Dimanche of Marseilles, in collaboration with the Harry Ransom Humanities Research Center. So far the following are available: *Don Juan et . . .* (1994), *Ecrits sur l' Art*, edited by Serge Fauchereau (1998) and the first instalment of the *Carnets*, covering some of the years in which Roché was 'Jim' and Franz Hessel was 'Jules', that is, *Carnets: Les Années Jules et Jim: Première Partie 1920–1921* (1990), with a preface by François Truffaut.

Linda Ashton has been the best of guides to the Roché papers. For the conception of *Free Spirits* I am deeply in debt to Alexandra Pringle and to Liz Calder, and for its writing to Marian McCarthy and Pascal Cariss. My research could not have been done without the help of Eileen MacKillop, my friends in Texas, Clare and Jack Ratliff, and Rikke Jensen and Alison Platt.

I am indebted to the Harry Ransom Humanities Research Center for a Mellon Fellowship and to the British Academy for grants in aid of research. For reproduction or translation of copyright material I am grateful to representatives of the 'Court' family, to Gallimard (Paris) and André Dimanche (Marseilles), to MK2 Productions, to the British Film Institute, and to Kika Markham.

A NOTE ON THE AUTHOR

IAN MACKILLOP is the author of *The British Ethical Societies*; *F.R. Leavis: A Life in Criticism* and *F.R. Leavis: Essays and Documents* (with Richard Storer). He is Reader in English at the University of Sheffield.

A NOTE ON THE TYPE

The text of this book is set in Linotype Sabon, named after the type founder, Jacques Sabon. It was designed by Jan Tschichold and jointly developed by Linotype, Monotype and Stempel, in response to a need for a typeface to be available in identical form for mechanical hot metal composition and hand composition using foundry type.

Tschichold based his design for Sabon roman on a fount engraved by Garamond, and Sabon italic on a fount by Granjon. It was first used in 1966 and has proved an enduring modern classic.